small scale

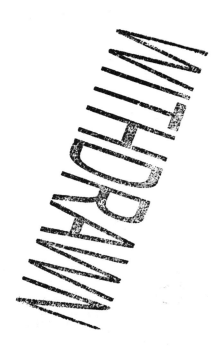

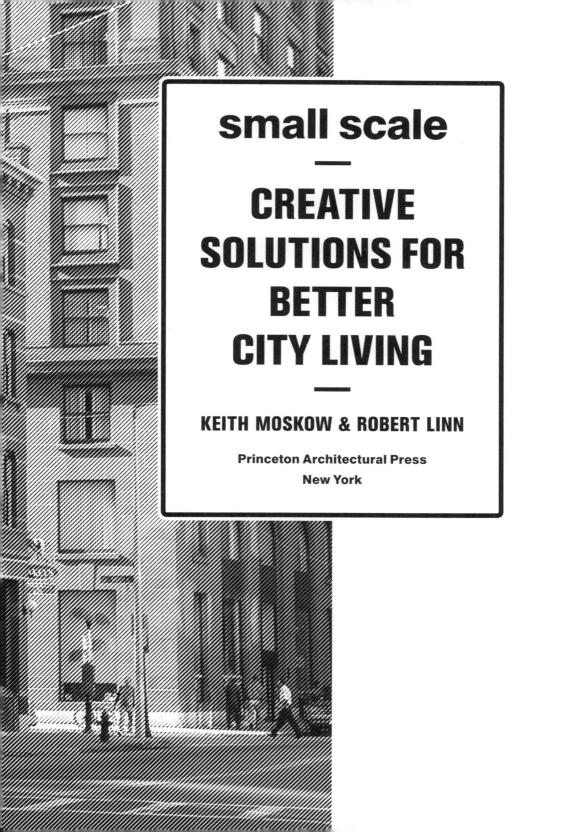

small scale

—

CREATIVE SOLUTIONS FOR BETTER CITY LIVING

—

KEITH MOSKOW & ROBERT LINN

Princeton Architectural Press

New York

CONTENTS

INSIGHT

DELIGHT

Published by
Princeton Architectural Press
37 East 7th Street, New York, NY 10003

For a free catalog of books call: 1-800-722-6657
Visit our website at: www.papress.com

Editor: Becca Casbon
Designer: Paul Wagner

Special thanks to: Nettie Aljian, Bree Anne Apperley,
Sara Bader, Nicola Bednarek, Janet Behning,
Carina Cha, Tom Cho, Penny (Yuen Pik) Chu,
Carolyn Deuschle, Russell Fernandez, Pete Fitzpatrick,
Jan Haux, Linda Lee, Laurie Manfra, John Myers,
Katharine Myers, Steve Royal, Dan Simon,
Andrew Stepanian, Jennifer Thompson, Joseph Weston,
and Deb Wood of Princeton Architectural Press
—Kevin C. Lippert, publisher

Library of Congress
Cataloging-in-Publication Data
Moskow, Keith.
Small scale : creative solutions for better city living /
Keith Moskow and Robert Linn. — 1st ed.
    p.   cm.
ISBN 978-1-56898-975-4 (alk. paper)
1. Public architecture. 2. Public spaces. 3.
Architecture—Human factors. 4. Architecture and
society. I. Linn, Robert (Robert Spencer), 1967–
II. Title. III. Title: Creative solutions for better
city living.
NA9050.5.M68 2010
724'.7—dc22
                        2010005106

ACKNOWLEDGMENTS

Thanks to the contributors of *Small Scale*, who supplied all the material for the book. Without their participation this publication would not be possible.

Thanks to our associate, Sarah West, who was the primary book organizer and worked with the contributors from around the world, managed the thousands of files submitted, and provided thoughtful insight into the book's development.

Thanks to Princeton Architectural Press, especially Becca Casbon and Jennifer Thompson, who believed in the relevance of *Small Scale* and shepherded the book through design and distribution.

And thanks to our families, including Allison, Erin, Zac, Jake, Jackson, and Ava, who are always supportive and are fellow cohabiters of our urban existence.

Keith Moskow and Robert Linn

INTRODUCTION

Eight years ago, while sailing on a friend's boat in Boston Harbor, we noticed a floating steel drydock that had washed up onto a beach in East Boston. The abandoned and decrepit ship-repair container had broken free from its moorings and drifted to the beach months before. Due to a complicated ownership history and liability issues, no one claimed any responsibility for the vessel. There it sat, blocking views and preventing residents from using their beach.

We immediately began brainstorming about how we might turn what the newspapers called a "rotting, hulking eyesore" into an asset. East Boston lacks green space, so on our own initiative (and nickel) we designed a sports facility that could be prefabricated and inserted into the drydock's rusting carcass. Where once there had been chipping paint, now there were soccer fields, bocce courts, children's play areas, public seating, and locker facilities. The success of this theoretical project led us from then on to regularly investigate schemes for making life better for city dwellers, and also led to the creation of this book, which collects small-scale urban interventions from architects around the world. [Figs. 1–3]

Urban interventions address the increasing density and limited availability of land in cities by identifying and using leftover urban spaces or voids or unrecognized tears in the city fabric. They are eminently achievable: they do not require years of permitting and government oversight, and they are not prohibitively expensive. These little architectural insertions do not require tremendous use of natural resources or whole-scale demolition and disposal of existing fabric, and suggest solutions to the larger problem of energy consumption. Similar to how microloans made to individuals in developing countries can improve the socioeconomic conditions of entire communities, these micro interventions hold the potential for a macro effect on an entire city.

1

2

3

4   5

More and more people are choosing to live and work in cities, seeking the stimulation and opportunity available only in an urban context. *Small Scale* contains case studies—ranging from purely conceptual to fully realized—that present visionary yet simple solutions to many specific needs inherent in contemporary urban life: places to contemplate, to find reprieve from urban intrusions, and to facilitate social interaction. Cities can be made better and more livable by employing innovative thinking to create easily do-able projects.

6

The projects in this book provide resources and amenities in the spirit of the best "street furniture" from various cultures, reminding us that urban invention is not a new idea. They build upon the tradition of such successful historical interventions as Japanese pocket gardens, the iconic red English telephone booths, the art nouveau Parisian subway entrances, and the pissoirs of Amsterdam. [Figs. 4–6] While taking inspiration from the past, the included works also reflect the promise of new materials and technologies—making ideas that were once the realm of science fiction into reality.

7

The abbreviated scope and budget of some of these projects allowed for a more hands-on, design-build approach. Often, younger, less-established firms—in their eagerness—have been able to make a significant contribution to the urban context with interventions. Playfulness and an entrepreneurial spirit enliven the included projects, straddling the gap between fantasy and reality, as well as art and architecture. These intriguing examples of intelligent design are decidedly not grand planning schemes or outrageously expensive public facilities. They instead focus on everyday human activities, while offering practical, sometimes humorous and ironic, means to improve the lives of city dwellers while enriching and enlivening the urban fabric. An example is Public Architecture's Day Labor Station (pp. 28–33). It provides a place for day laborers to wait for work in comfort, giving them a less transitory space in their community. [Fig. 7]

Small Scale is loosely organized into three sections based upon the projects' intentions: those that aim to provide a service, those that attempt to communicate insight, and those that simply delight. The service, or functional, category of interventions offers a response to a measurable need. The designers of these projects realized a gap in the utility of an area and designed a solution—providing services such as shade and cooling, nourishment, cleansing, and security. The projects in the "insightful" group share site-specific information and interpretation with the public in an effort to impart a more complete understanding of one's surroundings, focusing on education, discovery, and reflection. The interventions in the last section intend to delight public audiences by adding beauty, charm, play, and wit into the urban scene.

SERVICE

LA DALLMAN:
MARSUPIAL BRIDGE
MILWAUKEE, WISCONSIN

Program

Like many North American postindustrial cities, Milwaukee, Wisconsin, is replete with leftover interstitial spaces that are the by-products of urban infrastructure planned without engagement to its context. The multiphased Marsupial Bridge project involves the regeneration of such a zone, surrounding the 1925 Holton Street Viaduct that crosses the Milwaukee River. The viaduct is located in the heart of the densest neighborhood in southeastern Wisconsin, an emerging area for regeneration within a city that has experienced dramatic population loss since the middle of the twentieth century.

A coalition of neighborhood groups sought a transformative intervention to activate this brownfield, surrounded by neglected spaces, empty storefronts, abandoned industrial sites, and poorly planned traffic patterns. The project renews this unclaimed territory, offering the urban traveler a new vantage point from which to experience the viaduct as an engineered artifact and its residual terrain as a productive civic space.

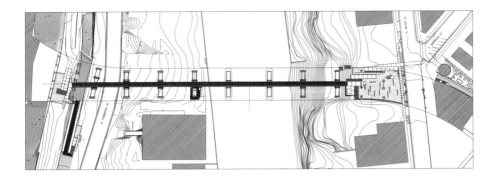

Solution

The project consists of multiple interwoven components along, within, and through the historic viaduct. A Media Garden acts as a civic connector and urban plaza, and a Marsupial Bridge offers a new pedestrian and bicycle connection. Additional interventions—including a bus shelter—preceded the bridge, and a moon-gazing platform is currently in progress.

The Media Garden converts an unsafe under-bridge area into a civic gathering space for film festivals, regattas, and other river events. The position of the Media Garden within the existing viaduct presented an unusual challenge due to the lack of natural daylight for plant growth. Accordingly, this area could not be defined through landscape design in the conventional sense; rather, concrete benches are set amidst a moonscape of gravel and seating boulders. By day, the benches provide a respite for pedestrians and bicyclists as they make their way across the Marsupial Bridge. By night, the benches are lit from within, transforming the plaza into a beacon for the neighborhood. This strategy challenges the traditional notion of public space as a "town square" or "village green," and provides a site-specific program for the under-bridge zone.

The Marsupial Bridge weaves through the viaduct, using the existing structure as its "host." The viaduct was originally engineered to support trolley cars, a transportation system that was abandoned due to increased automobile use in the early 1900s. The Marsupial Bridge hangs opportunistically from the over-structured middle-third section of the viaduct, responding to changing transportation needs of the city for greater pedestrian and bicycle connections. The bridge is a "green highway" that activates the unused space beneath the viaduct, encourages alternative forms of transportation, and connects residential neighborhoods to natural amenities, Milwaukee's downtown, and the Brady Street commercial district. The Marsupial Bridge's undulating concrete deck offers a counterpoint to the existing steel members of the viaduct, inspired by the notion of weaving a new spine through the structure. Floor lighting is integrated behind the apron, and precision theatrical fixtures are mounted above, creating a localized ribbon of illumination with minimal spill into the riparian landscape below.

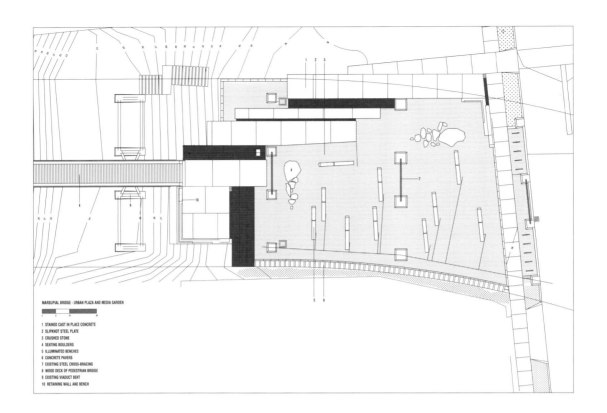

MARSUIPIAL BRIDGE - URBAN PLAZA AND MEDIA GARDEN

1 STAINED CAST IN PLACE CONCRETE
2 SLIPKNOT STEEL PLATE
3 CRUSHED STONE
4 SEATING BOULDERS
5 ILLUMINATED BENCHES
6 CONCRETE PAVERS
7 EXISTING STEEL CROSS-BRACING
8 WOOD DECK OF PEDESTRIAN BRIDGE
9 EXISTING VIADUCT BENT
10 RETAINING WALL AND BENCH

MOSKOW LINN ARCHITECTS: ZIPCAR DISPENSER

BOSTON, MASSACHUSETTS

Program

Zipcar is a car-sharing company with locations in more than fifty cities in North America and the United Kingdom. The Zipcar business plan offers a new model for on-demand, internet-reserved automobile transportation. Each Zipcar is said to replace seven to ten privately owned cars, lowering both driving and parking congestion and reducing greenhouse gas emissions.

Solution

The Zipcar Dispenser offers a solution to the company's biggest problem: locating parking spaces available for lease in the dense urban areas where their vehicles are most needed. The dispenser is a self-serve, mechanized, stacked parking prototype for Zipcar, similar to a giant PEZ dispenser. Here, cars are doled out in lieu of candy. The design allows for seven Zipcars to be stacked in the same area as two tandem nine-by-eighteen-foot parking spaces. At the time of the dispenser's conception, all cars leased by Zipcar were Volkswagen Beetles, eliminating any need for consideration of customer selection or sorting.

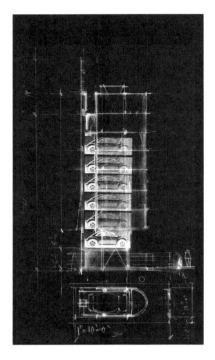

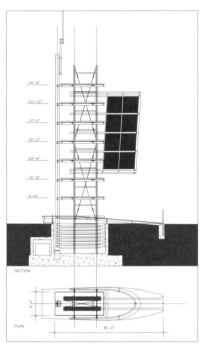

Once a Zipcar member inserts their membership card into the dispenser's card reader, a translucent shroud lowers to the street level, protecting the person from the project's mechanics. As the shroud rises, a car is deposited—ready for use. The procedure works in reverse when the car is returned. Additionally, the tower maximizes Zipcar's presence in the city by providing a recognizable symbol for the emerging company, and may serve as a canvas for billboard-type advertising.

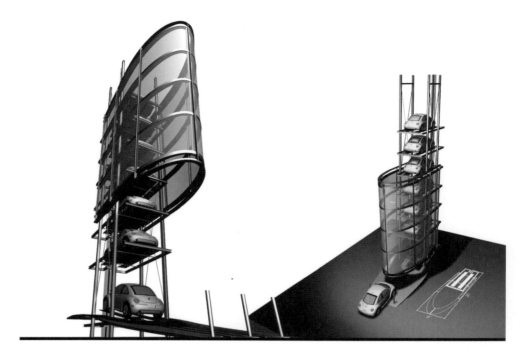

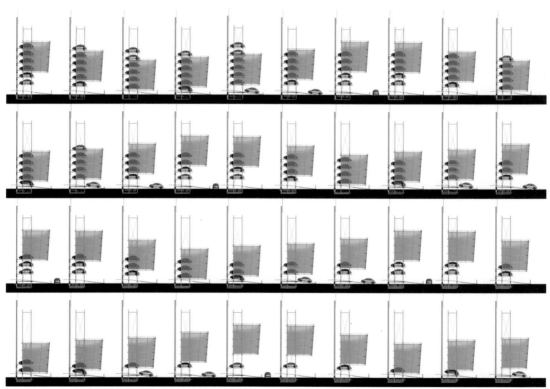

GROUND: SUPERNATURAL

VANCOUVER, BRITISH COLUMBIA

Program

SuperNatural is located on three adjacent roadway intersections along Garden Drive in Vancouver, British Columbia. While normally a quiet residential street, because of its proximity to two heavy-commuting arterial routes, Garden Drive had become a popular vehicular "cut through" during rush hour. A two-stage design competition sponsored by the city of Vancouver's Public Art Program called for the creation of three small roundabouts to act as traffic-calming devices that would slow cars down, provide safe pedestrian crossings, and deter commuter shortcuts.

Solution

The project takes as its departure the double meaning implied in the phrase "Super, Natural British Columbia"—the slogan of the province's tourism campaign. Recognizing the paradox of Vancouver's identification with an ideal image of raw nature, even while being a dense city, Ground designed SuperNatural to let the crudeness of rock and the infrastructure of the city intensify each other through a somewhat uncomfortable adjacency.

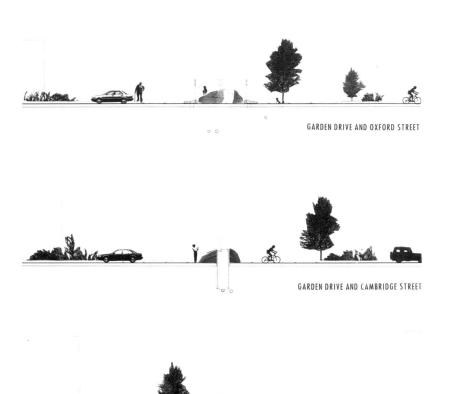

GARDEN DRIVE AND OXFORD STREET

GARDEN DRIVE AND CAMBRIDGE STREET

GARDEN DRIVE AND ETON STREET

The supernatural, or unnatural, contiguity of the natural and urban is emphasized by a minimal installation strategy. At two of the intersections, twenty-ton boulders seem to have been dropped haphazardly in the middle of the road. At the third intersection, a boulder sits in a field of ornamental grass ringed by a concrete circle. Despite their seemingly alien interruption of the streetscape, the massive rocks are carefully designed elements of the traffic system. Due to a combination of height, proportion, and facet angles, the rocks interrupt views, slow and reorganize traffic patterns, yet still accommodate pedestrian and vehicular visibility as determined by city guidelines.

The boulders of SuperNatural sit within a grid of traffic reflectors, common elements of city streets that in this project signal the areas for pedestrian crossing and mark the zone of artistic intervention. In contrast to the obdurate immobility of the massive rocks, the "keep right" signs were deliberately given a provisional character, as though hastily installed as warning signs, further suggesting the oddity of the rocks' arrival in the midst of the city.

PUBLIC ARCHITECTURE: DAY LABOR STATION
PROTOTYPE DESIGN

Program

Each day, more than 110,000 people look for day labor work in the United States. Over 75 percent of day labor hiring sites occupy spaces meant for other uses, such as street corners and home improvement store parking lots. Due in part to their visibility, day laborers are often seen as symbols of the country's broken immigration system and its increasing dependence on a low-wage, contingent workforce. Some residents, businesses, city officials, and police have attempted to address the issues by marginalizing and criminalizing day laborers seeking work. This deflects attention from the real issue day laborers face: their lack of integration into the community.

Solution

Design is often viewed as a luxury, and yet it can be used as a tool with greater impact and longevity than a political statement or a judicial ruling. The Day Labor Station is a prototypical solution—designed to be a model that can be replicated by anyone—that provides an innovative vehicle through which to advance the status of day laborers within the community. As the clients, day laborers are involved in the planning, building, and maintenance of each station.

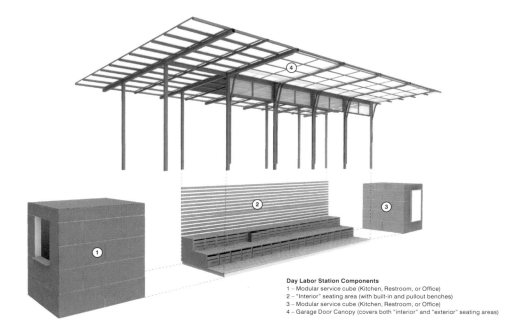

Day Labor Station Components
1 – Modular service cube (Kitchen, Restroom, or Office)
2 – "Interior" seating area (with built-in and pullout benches)
3 – Modular service cube (Kitchen, Restroom, or Office)
4 – Garage Door Canopy (covers both "interior" and "exterior" seating areas)

The station provides a sheltered space to wait for work as well as restroom facilities. The open nature of the seating area is designed to provide maximum visual contact between workers and potential employers. For the workers, this visual contact is key to their perception of a fair hiring process. While green materials and strategies help achieve a minimal environmental footprint, the station also addresses issues of social and economic sustainability, acting as employment center, classroom, and meeting space. In addition, it can contain a kitchen, to provide an income-generating food business, or, if preferable, a small office for administrative functions.

By giving laborers a more dignified presence in the public realm, the station and accompanying advocacy initiative elevate the debate about the workers' role within the fabric of the community.

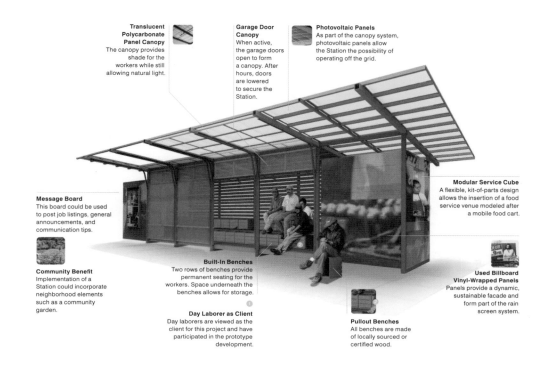

Translucent Polycarbonate Panel Canopy
The canopy provides shade for the workers while still allowing natural light.

Garage Door Canopy
When active, the garage doors open to form a canopy. After hours, doors are lowered to secure the Station.

Photovoltaic Panels
As part of the canopy system, photovoltaic panels allow the Station the possibility of operating off the grid.

Message Board
This board could be used to post job listings, general announcements, and communication tips.

Community Benefit
Implementation of a Station could incorporate neighborhood elements such as a community garden.

Built-In Benches
Two rows of benches provide permanent seating for the workers. Space underneath the benches allows for storage.

Day Laborer as Client
Day laborers are viewed as the client for this project and have participated in the prototype development.

Modular Service Cube
A flexible, kit-of-parts design allows the insertion of a food service venue modeled after a mobile food cart.

Used Billboard Vinyl-Wrapped Panels
Panels provide a dynamic, sustainable facade and form part of the rain screen system.

Pullout Benches
All benches are made of locally sourced or certified wood.

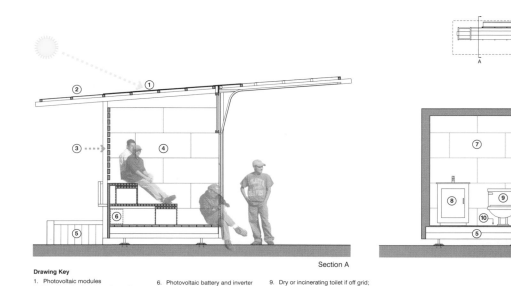

Section A

Section B

Drawing Key

1. Photovoltaic modules
2. Translucent polycarbonate panels
3. Air flow through seating area
4. Used billboard vinyl wrapped panels
5. Locally sourced, salvaged, or certified wood (used throughout the Station)

6. Photovoltaic battery and inverter location
7. Fiber cement panels
8. Sink with low flow fixtures (Undersink greywater filtration system can be linked with toilet if needed.)

9. Dry or incinerating toilet if off grid; low flow toilet if on the grid
10. Recycled PVC floor tile

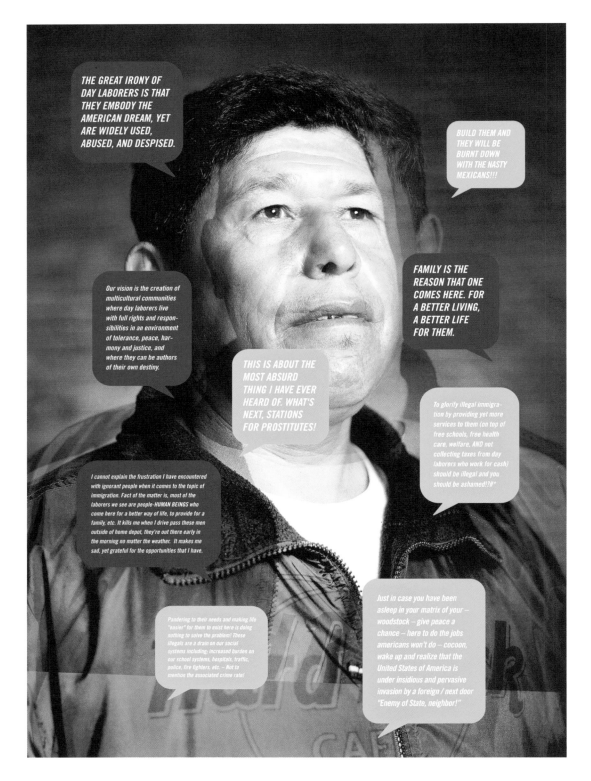

Restroom
Toilet facilities are a basic yet critical need often lacking at most informal sites. In situations where there is a larger day laborer population, the flexibility of the Station's design concept allows for more than one restroom cube.

Office
Day laborers are highly organized. The Station not only has the potential to host meetings, but in situations where the day laborers desire a coordinator, a cube can be designed as an office.

Kitchen
The kitchen can function as a food business, serving as an income generator for the Station as well as a food service training opportunity for workers. With employers as well as patrons from nearby businesses as customers, it also provides a focal point for social interaction.

→ **A retractable pedestrian drawbridge**

HEATHERWICK STUDIO: ROLLING BRIDGE
LONDON, UNITED KINGDOM

Program

Rolling Bridge, part of a five-hundred-million-pound development of Paddington Basin in Central London, came from a commission for a pedestrian bridge to sit across an inlet of the Grand Union Canal and provide an access route for workers and residents. Crucially, the bridge needed to open to allow boats moored in the inlet to sail in and out.

Solution

Rather than being a single, rigid element that fractures to allow river traffic through, Heatherwick Studio's Rolling Bridge opens by slowly and smoothly curling up, transforming from a conventional pedestrian platform into a circular sculpture that sits on the bank of the canal. The studio's aim was to make the bridge's function and movement its extraordinary aspects. With this in mind, the architects kept the bridge's design simple, leaving its real identity hidden until it starts moving.

34

The structure opens using a series of hydraulic rams set into the timber platform of the bridge. As it curls, each of its eight segments simultaneously lifts, causing it to roll until the two ends touch and form a circle. The bridge can be stopped at any point along its journey, whether at the very start, when it looks as though it is hovering, or halfway through its opening path. The Rolling Bridge opens and closes a number of times each week, including every Friday at midday.

Engineering firm SKM Anthony Hunts collaborated with Heatherwick Studio on the project from its conception. The whole structure was built at Littlehampton Welding on the Sussex coast and then floated up the Grand Union Canal, before being lifted into position over the canal, where it was attached to the mechanics that power its movement.

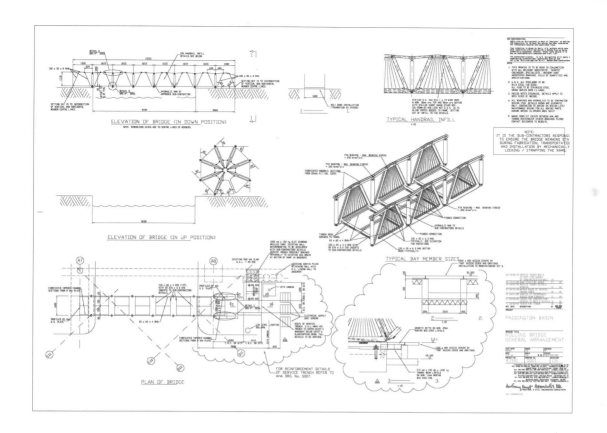

ELEVATION OF BRIDGE (IN DOWN POSITION)

TYPICAL HANDRAIL INFILL

ELEVATION OF BRIDGE (IN UP POSITION)

TYPICAL BAY MEMBER SIZES

PLAN OF BRIDGE

PADDINGTON BASIN

ROLLING BRIDGE
GENERAL ARRANGEMENT

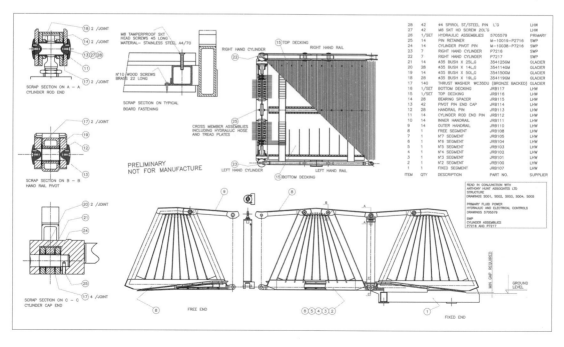

SCRAP SECTION ON A – A
CYLINDER ROD END

SCRAP SECTION ON TYPICAL
BOARD FASTENING

SCRAP SECTION ON B – B
HAND RAIL PIVOT

PRELIMINARY
NOT FOR MANUFACTURE

SCRAP SECTION ON C – C
CYLINDER CAP END

ITEM	QTY	DESCRIPTION	PART NO.	SUPPLIER
28	42	#4 SPIROL ST/STEEL PIN L'G		LHW
27	42	M8 SKT HD SCREW 20L'G		LHW
26	1/SET	HYDRAULIC ASSEMBLIES	S705579	PRIMARY
25	14	PIN RETAINER	M–10019–P7216	SWP
24	14	CYLINDER PIVOT PIN	M–10038–P7216	SWP
23	7	RIGHT HAND CYLINDER	P7216	SWP
22	7	RIGHT HAND CYLINDER	P7217	SWP
21	14	#35 BUSH X 25L,G	354125GM	GLACIER
20	28	#35 BUSH X 14L,G	354114GM	GLACIER
19	14	#35 BUSH X 50L,G	354150GM	GLACIER
18	28	#35 BUSH X 19L,G	354119GM	GLACIER
17	140	THRUST WASHER WC35DU (BRONZE BACKED)		GLACIER
16	1/SET	BOTTOM DECKING	JRB117	LHW
15	1/SET	TOP DECKING	JRB116	LHW
14	28	BEARING SPACER	JRB115	LHW
13	42	PIVOT PIN END CAP	JRB114	LHW
12	14	CYLINDER ROD END PIN	JRB113	LHW
11	14	HANDRAIL PIN	JRB112	LHW
10	14	INNER HANDRAIL	JRB111	LHW
9	14	OUTER HANDRAIL	JRB110	LHW
8	1	FREE SEGMENT	JRB108	LHW
7	1	N°7 SEGMENT	JRB105	LHW
6	1	N°6 SEGMENT	JRB104	LHW
5	1	N°5 SEGMENT	JRB103	LHW
4	1	N°4 SEGMENT	JRB102	LHW
3	1	N°3 SEGMENT	JRB101	LHW
2	1	N°2 SEGMENT	JRB100	LHW
1	1	FIXED SEGMENT	JRB107	LHW

READ IN CONJUNCTION WITH
ANTHONY HUNT ASSOCIATES LTD
STRUCTURE
DRAWINGS S001, S002, S003, S004, S005

PRIMARY FLUID POWER
HYDRAULIC AND ELECTRICAL CONTROLS
DRAWINGS S705579

SWP
CYLINDER ASSEMBLIES
P7216 AND P7217

ROGERS MARVEL ARCHITECTS: TIGERTRAP
PROTOTYPE DESIGN

Program

In today's world, critical buildings and public sites often require perimeter security. The American landscape is historically unaccustomed to the tyranny of security devices—our dense urban spaces grudgingly accommodate the traditionally cumbersome engineered solutions to force protection criteria. The architecture of security should be a design problem as much as a technical problem. Rock 12 Security Architecture and Rogers Marvel Architects designed the TigerTrap as a holistic solution to provide a point of balance between engineered protection and an inhabitable public realm.

Solution

The TigerTrap is an innovative concept designed to reduce the visual impact of force protection installations on public space. It employs subgrade, compressible concrete in conjunction with pedestrian amenities such as benches, low site walls, or earthworks. The compressible concrete is carefully calibrated to withstand pedestrian loads, but fail under the weight of a vehicle. By lowering the elevation and speed of a vehicular threat, barrier strategies may be minimized. For sites with enough dimension, the barrier strategy that accompanies the TigerTrap may be constructed completely below ground level, eliminating all visible aboveground security elements. The system has been tested with a variety of surfaces, such as cobblestone paving and a vegetative lawn, both configured to accommodate foot traffic.

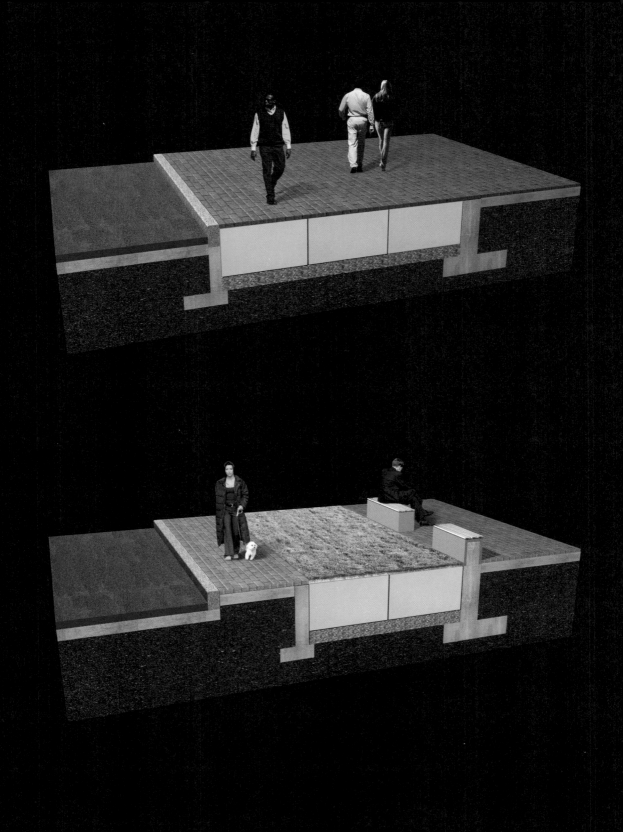

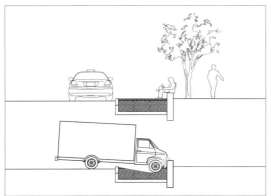

The TigerTrap is a custom product, designed specifically for each site. A prototype installation, developed in cooperation with the Engineered Arresting Systems Corporation, is currently installed in Battery Park City in New York City, protecting the New York Mercantile Exchange and the World Financial Center.

ECOSISTEMA URBANO ARQUITECTOS: ECOBOULEVARD
VALLECAS, SPAIN

Program

Vallecas, Spain, is a poorly planned suburban neighborhood. The Ecoboulevard competition was organized with two objectives: to generate social activity in the neighborhood and to make a bioclimatic outdoor space. Public spaces belong to everyone, and they should support a variety of activities and events, allowing people to act freely and spontaneously.

Solution

Ecosistema Urbano Arquitectos proposed Ecoboulevard to make up for the lack of social activity in Vallecas due to irresponsible planning. The firm believed that the best adaptation for a public space would be to add thick, solid trees, but these would take fifteen or twenty years to grow large enough to make an impact. Instead, the architects created an "emergency" intervention that could operate immediately in the same way that trees would in the future. The firm opted for a strategy of concentration that acts on and adapts specific parts of the neighborhood, making these areas the seeds of a public-space regeneration process.

Ecoboulevard consists of three pavilions, which act as frameworks for multiple activities chosen by their users. These pavilions perform the following functions: defining social spaces in an existing, but unused, large public area; providing shade and respite from the sun; and reducing and reorganizing the asymmetric arrangement of vehicular traffic circulation. Installed in Vallecas as temporary prostheses, the pavilions will be used only until the neighborhood's inactivity and climatic adaptation problems are corrected. Once the necessary time has elapsed, these devices should be taken down, and their former sites should remain as clearings in the wood.

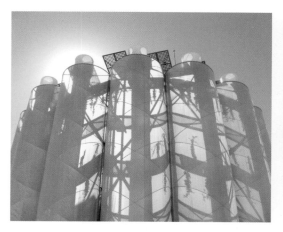

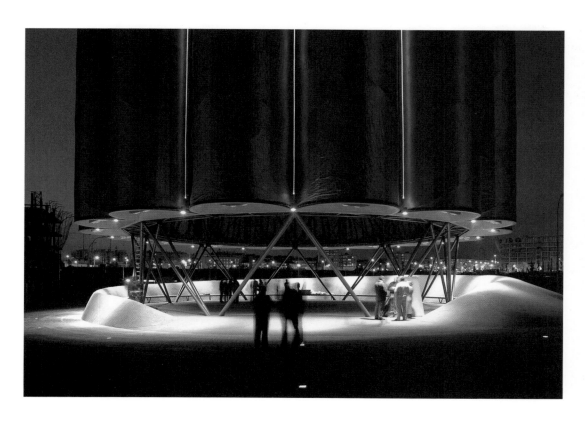

SERVICE

MACHADO AND SILVETTI ASSOCIATES: DEWEY SQUARE MBTA HEAD HOUSES
BOSTON, MASSACHUSETTS

Program
Dewey Square is a public plaza in Boston's Financial District with sizeable, privately owned plazas abutting it. A privately funded redesign of the square and surrounding plazas, in conjunction with the city's Central Artery/Tunnel Project, called for the entire area, public and private plazas, to be reconceived as one urban space with a single contemporary character, unique within the city.

Solution
In attempting to maintain the space as a distinctive, inclusive, and progressive public plaza, Machado and Silvetti Associates created a condition of orchestrated variety through several components. The square's overall pavement serves as a continuous carpet of stone and concrete, onto which a series of disparate objects are placed. The pavement's patterns reflect the large scale of the plaza, with a giant order of stripes that adjust in width to accommodate the different objects. Each object is carefully aligned in order to establish visual relationships with the main pedestrian thresholds into the square.

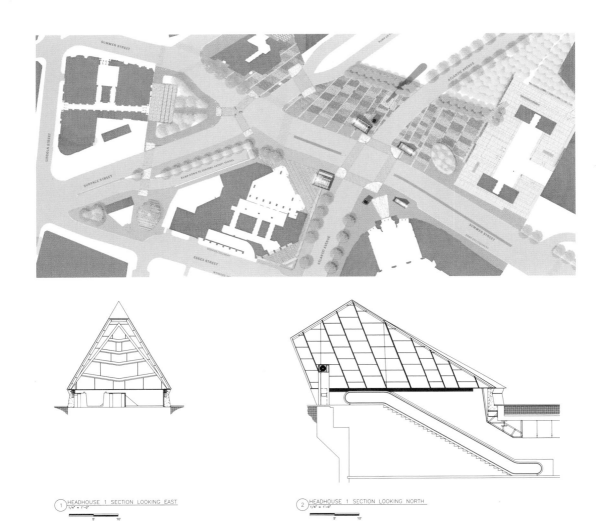

The glass-louvered MBTA (Massachusetts Bay Transportation Authority) subway entrance pavilions lead to underground train access, give the Dewey Square precinct a distinctive identity, and serve as glowing beacons at night. The glass lobbies of the surrounding office buildings inspired the concept behind these struc-tures, with the completed head houses acting as a public version of these private spaces, in order to support urban activities in the newly revitalized Dewey Square.

DESIGNLAB:
PARASOL AND LIGHT ROOMS
BOSTON, MASSACHUSETTS

Program

Seasonal affective disorder (SAD) is a condition that more than ten million Americans suffer from, and many more worldwide, with the highest incidence in northern latitudes. Researchers believe that therapy using bright light can lift depression or reset a sleep cycle. DesignLAB proposed two solutions—paraSOL and Light Rooms—to provide respite from the darkness of winter.

Solution / paraSOL

The paraSOL is a personal nimbus for the modern city dweller. A unique, iconic accessory with a solid grounding in practical necessity, paraSOL makes a striking fashion statement in even the worst of weather. Powered by motion-sensitive, piezoelectric material on its waterproof top surface, paraSOL emits full-spectrum light from its underside, using a lightweight, electroluminescent fabric. The harder it rains, the brighter the underside shines, bringing light to an otherwise dark day.

One paraSOL offers a break in the clouds, a single halo; several create a hearth, a space for gathering that suffuses its occupants with warmth. ParaSOL makes the rain a reason to stay outside and talk. Users are drawn to one another and rainy day friendships are formed.

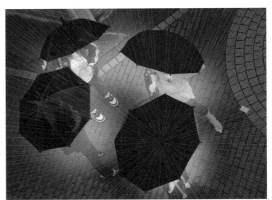

Solution / Light Rooms

Light Rooms are constructed of translucent polycarbonate panels, enclosing simple benches for up to twelve people. A full-spectrum, ten-thousand-lux light source bounces light off one opaque wall, simultaneously flooding the interior with light and creating a glowing neighborhood beacon. The result is happiness!

→ **An urban bench built with interlocking blocks to define an outdoor room**

ZAHA HADID ARCHITECTS: URBAN NEBULA

LONDON, UNITED KINGDOM

Solution

By combining traditional, repetitive precast molding techniques with contemporary computer numerical control (CNC) machine molding, Zaha Hadid Architects created a system of standard elements in which each individual component has a unique variation. Taking its name from the form of a nebula gas, the individual elements of the piece create a fluidity that resonates with the structure of a nebula, yet presents an enigmatic contradiction by being made of concrete— a material typically perceived to be inert. Areas of darkness and light visible in a nebula are evident within the Urban Nebula as hexagonal and triangular voids produced by the positioning of the installation's individual elements.

Program

Urban Nebula was created by Zaha Hadid Architects for the 2007 London Design Festival. Its intent was to visualize precast concrete as a building material that could allow new formal expression of fluidity and seamlessness, while adding a strong poetic quality to the urban space of the city.

The 8-by-37-by-15-foot installation is composed of 150 blocks of black, polished precast concrete with a total mass of 30 tons, bolted together to form a perforated wall that seamlessly transforms into furniture, resonating between architecture as a material system and sculptural form. Urban Nebula is reminiscent of the rough, improvisational characteristics of dry stone walling (the construction of a wall of interlocking stones without any mortar), yet adopts the smooth, polished surface of stone pebbles in a riverbed.

The original design of one standard element with a range of end conditions was mapped using three-dimensional imaging software. The individual elements were then made using standard steel molds into which computer-cut polystyrene end pieces were inserted, together with stainless-steel anchors for fixing. "In a design environment dominated by new software enabling us to rethink form and space radically, there is always continued development of materials that match our computer-generated complex shapes and spatial conditions. We aim for an expansion of the material's performance and try not to think in the limits that are given to a certain material by conventional applications. These new manufacturing processes play an important role in the architectural language of fluidity and porosity evident in our work, and an essential element in the sculptural sensuality of the piece," states Hadid. "The complexity of Urban Nebula's casting regime and extreme form of construction were an exciting challenge for all involved."

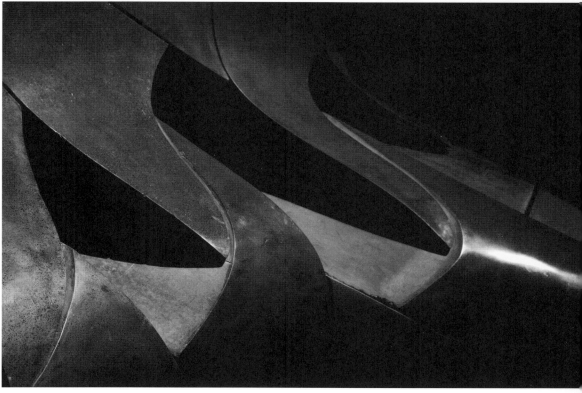

In their quest to address the underlying problem of constructing free-form architecture, Zaha Hadid Architects worked with Aggregate Industries to explore the plastic qualities of concrete. Aggregate Industries' experience in precision construction, molding techniques, and mix design enabled a high level of experimentation—producing intense color with exceptionally high dimensional tolerance and surface finish across the individual concrete elements of Urban Nebula.

MOSKOW LINN ARCHITECTS: RIVER GENIE

PROTOTYPE URBAN RIVER CLEANSER

Solution

The River Genie's design is based on the integration of the Native American seine fishing net and the Playtex Diaper Genie. The River Genie vessel is moored to the floor of a river and oriented against the current. Floating garbage is skimmed off the surface of the water and funneled into an expandable net, which is monitored and replaced when full. Escape louvers positioned at the mouth of the net prevent the entrapment of aquatic life. Pontoons, located on either side of the vessel, consist of a translucent eco-resin shell supported by a rigid frame. At night, the pontoons are lit from within by solar-powered LED fixtures, emitting a soft glow much like floating Japanese lanterns to warn passing boats of their presence. The River Genie was designed as a theoretical project and won the gold medal at the 2008 Seoul Design Olympiad.

Program

Each year, millions of tons of garbage float down rivers worldwide. The most highly concentrated amounts are in and around urban areas. Floating garbage pollutes water sources, is hazardous to both marine and avian wildlife, and is visually unappealing. The River Genie passively collects these disagreeable elements from the aquatic environment.

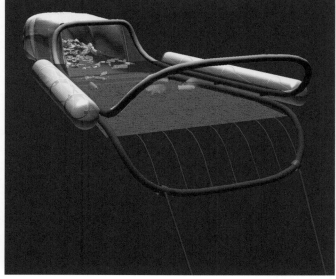

ATELIER BOW-WOW: WHITE LIMOUSINE YATAI
NIIGATA, JAPAN

Program

A Japanese *yatai* (street cart) serves food from the side of the road, and has a wonderful charm that brings people together and encourages interaction. The standard yatai is about five feet long and is run by one person. Inspired by this phenomenon, Atelier Bow-Wow designed a "limousine yatai."

Solution

The White Limousine Yatai stretches to become thirty-three feet long, enabling more people to gather around it and elevating its urban appeal. It was displayed at the 2003 Echigo-Tsumari Art Triennial in Niigata, Japan. The long yatai, painted all white, visited various events and made a micro public space. Every time it turned a street corner it created a small traffic jam, but its humorous appearance made people laugh. As reference to the heavy snow in the area where the festival was held, the architects selected white or translucent local food specialities (Japanese rice wine, tofu, pickled white radishes) to be served from the yatai.

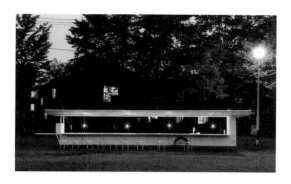
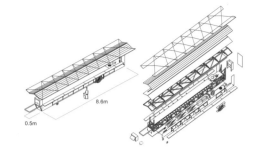

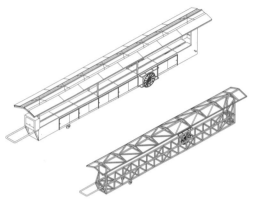

0.5m

8.6m

```
┌─────────────────────────────────────┐
│                                     │
│            BOORA:                   │
│       TEMPORARY EVENT               │
│          COMPLEX                    │
│        PORTLAND, OREGON             │
│                                     │
└─────────────────────────────────────┘
```

Program:

The Temporary Event Complex was created for the Portland Institute for Contemporary Art (PICA) 2005 Time-Based Art Festival, which brings contemporary performing and visual artists to the city for ten days of performances, expositions, salons, workshops, and discourse. At the end of each day of the festival, artists and audience members decamp to The Works, a late-night destination offering food, lounges, cabaret, studio theater, music, and dance performances. Each year, PICA looks for a different location for The Works, and challenges a pro bono design team to create an innovative temporary installation to house it.

Boora's design for The Works was built on a full-block site in a small-scale commercial section of Portland's Northwest neighborhood. A nineteenth-century structure—originally used as a Wells Fargo stagecoach depot, stable, and hayloft—sits on the eastern half of the site, while a shipping and receiving warehouse—with an elevated loading dock, loading bays, and overhead warehouse doors—shares the western half of the site with an asphalt service yard.

Solution:

The enclosed, high-volume, and clear-span natures of the former stagecoach and warehouse buildings made them logical choices for the locations of a one-hundred-seat studio theater and a cabaret performance space, respectively. An antechamber leading to the theater space became a lobby with the addition of seating, video installations, and beverage services. On the asphalt service yard on the opposite side of the site, a scaffolding structure wrapped in orange construction fencing and a canvas concert canopy provided shelter for a covered garden for large crowds. Nearby, the overhead doors of the warehouse cabaret could be opened or closed in a variety of ways, providing different options for enclosing the cabaret and allowing its sounds to escape to the outside. At the rear of the warehouse cabaret, adjacent to at-grade warehouse loading bays that became a restaurant, a beer garden—open to the sky but softened by potted trees—provided seating and alfresco dining and drinking. A construction fencing–clad scaffold wall at the back of the beer garden concealed portable toilets and a service/food-preparation area.

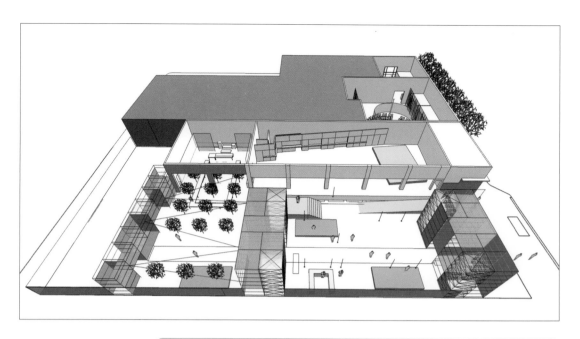

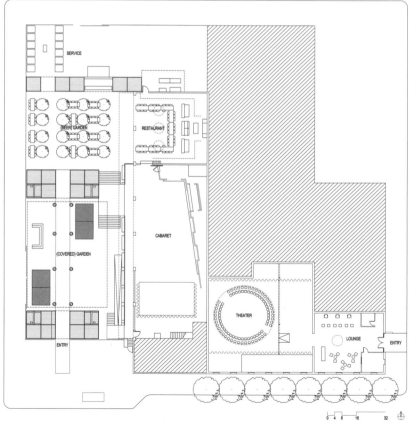

SERVICE

(BEER) GARDEN

RESTAURANT

(COVERED) GARDEN

CABARET

THEATER

LOUNGE

ENTRY

ENTRY

0 4 8   16   32

TEMPORARY EVENT COMPLEX

JOSEF PAUL KLEIHUES
FOR WALL AG: CITY-PISSOIR
BERLIN, DÜSSELDORF, AND MÜNSTER, GERMANY

Program

Between 1997 and 2004, architect Josef Paul Kleihues designed a number of units for international street furniture provider and outdoor advertiser Wall AG. One of these units is the City-Pissoir, a public urinal that is part of the product family "streetline," which was developed especially for inner-city areas. Kleihues created streetline in 1997, and City-Pissoirs have since been set up in the German cities of Berlin, Düsseldorf, and Münster.

Solution

Most of the street furniture developed by Kleihues follows the principle of type and model, which allows for the production of families or series of street furniture units. The City-Pissoir is a clean affair, requiring minimum space. With its small surface area and discreet design, it adapts itself easily to the existing cityscape. In highly frequented areas like train stations and shopping malls, it helps solve the problem of public urination.

The interior of the pissoir contains a washroom and a urinal, separated by a frosted glass pane. The washroom has a hand basin with a sensor-controlled cold water outlet, soap dispenser, and automatic hand dryer, ensuring water conservation and touch-free usage of the washroom's fittings. The interior walls of the urinal are made of polished stainless-steel sheeting, the floor consists of checker plates, and the ceiling is a backlit, light-frosted security glass pane. Two sensor-controlled flush nozzles are mounted above the urinal channel.

The framework of the pissoir consists of powder-coated, extruded aluminum. The outer shell of the urinal is formed by two display cases, which not only provide an advantageous presentation of advertising or information, but also an additional exterior illumination of the pissoir at night.

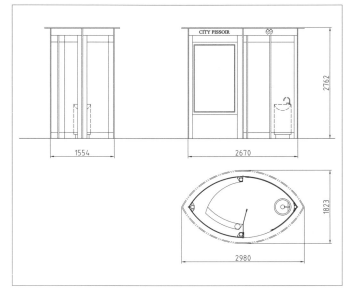

MOSKOW LINN ARCHITECTS: URBAN HOOKAH

BOSTON, MASSACHUSETTS

Program

"No Smoking" laws have removed the environmental hazards of secondhand smoke from within buildings, but the resulting effect is smokers loitering around alcoves and entryways. These fugitive smokers have a negative effect on the psyche of the street.

Solution

The Urban Hookah—which could be installed adjacent to restaurants, offices, commercial buildings, or any other place where smoking is prohibited—benefits the general public by filtering smoke and providing an integral ashtray. It is an "oasis" of defined sidewalk real estate for displaced smokers.

Consisting of a prefabricated kiosk, the Urban Hookah is shaped to partially enclose the user, with a heating and air-filtration system, lighter, and trash receptacle. It can be attached to any urban lamppost using its universal clamping collar—and removed as needs change. Existing electric service brings power to the heating coils, which are sheathed in a fiberglass shell. The shell wraps around the pole to create a radiant heat "jacket." Concealed within this jacket is an air-filtration system that draws smoke up and out the top of the structure, along with a receptacle for used butts. A polycarbonate armature fastened to the structural frame provides shelter from the sun, rain, and wind. The space accommodates two or three smokers.

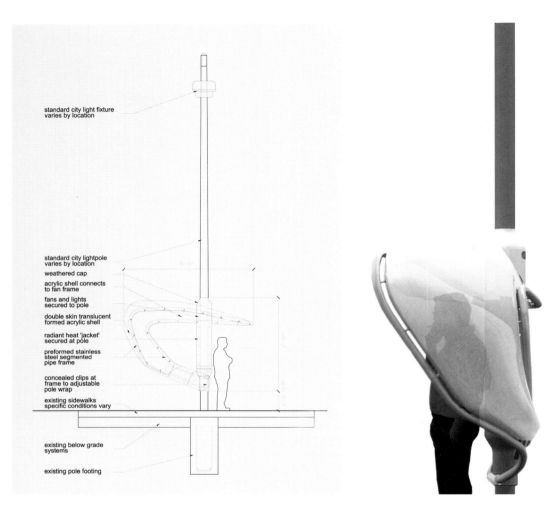

standard city light fixture
varies by location

standard city lightpole
varies by location

weathered cap

acrylic shell connects
to fan frame

fans and lights
secured to pole

double skin translucent
formed acrylic shell

radiant heat 'jacket'
secured at pole

preformed stainless
steel segmented
pipe frame

concealed clips at
frame to adjustable
pole wrap

existing sidewalks
specific conditions vary

existing below grade
systems

existing pole footing

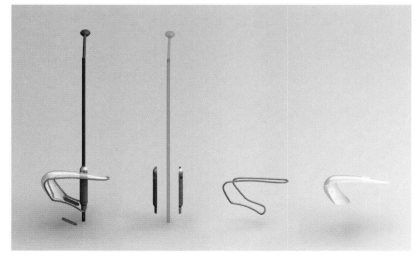

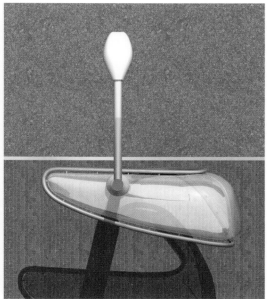

→ **A lobby relocated to the exterior**

MORPHOSIS:
CALTRANS DISTRICT 7
HEADQUARTERS PUBLIC PLAZA
LOS ANGELES, CALIFORNIA

Program

The new headquarters for District 7 of Caltrans (California Department of Transportation) is located in downtown Los Angeles. A public plaza was designed to be an outdoor lobby as well as an integral element of the headquarters. The plaza intensifies the circulation and encourages productive social exchange for both the Caltrans staff and the public.

Solution

The plaza's organizational strategy and the building's public interior were informed by an optimistic assessment of the vibrancy that will occur as the nearby urban environment develops further. Morphosis relocated Caltrans's main lobby to the exterior, as a large plaza for office workers, visitors, and the general public. Amenities, including an exhibition gallery and cafeteria, adjoin the outdoor lobby at ground level to draw users from pedestrian and vehicular traffic.

78

SERVICE

CALIFORNIA DEPARTMENT OF TRANSPORTATION

The project's entire budget for public art was invested in one installation—designed in collaboration with artist Keith Sonnier—that integrates inseparably with the architecture. Horizontal bands of red neon and blue argon light tubes cycle through light pattern sequences, mimicking the ribbons of headlights on California's freeways. The large, cantilevered light-bar connects the structure to First Street, while a forty-foot, forward-canted super-graphic "100" marks the South Main Street entrance. This layered sign, with its nod to Los Angeles's Hollywood sign, denotes the building as an urban landmark.

MIDWEST ARCHITECTURE STUDIO: MVG RETAIL PAVILIONS
PROTOTYPE DESIGN

Program

MVG is a real estate, design, and manufac-turing company whose goal is to rethink the franchise model of large, expensive, stand-alone stores for national brands. In every urban and suburban area, there are underutilized spaces in high-traffic (foot and vehicle) locations that are too small for a traditional store, but big enough for a walk-up or drive-through retail pavilion. These spaces tend to become blemishes in the visual fabric due to their noncon-forming size. Populating these sites offers consumers greater convenience, improves the aesthetic of the vacant spaces, and blurs the boundaries between manufactur-ing and construction.

Solution

MVG plans to find the best small-scale real estate sites and offer them to retail brands, complete with smartly designed, boldly customized, and efficiently manufactured and installed pavilions. The economic inspiration for the pavilions comes from the many drive-through-only coffee shops of the Pacific Northwest. The pavilions' design provides an environmentally smart use of materials, resources, land, and time. They can be efficiently mass-produced off-site from modular components similar to a manufactured product, then quickly shipped and installed on small-footprint sites. The production of each unit takes advantage of digital technology, with a custom-modular approach to design and fabrication centered on a three-component system: core (common to all unit types), accessories (product-specific components), and cladding (brand-specific identity).

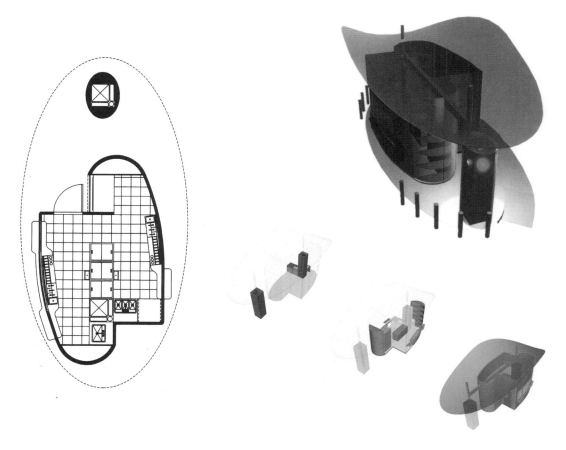

JULIE SNOW AND MATTHEW KREILICH: CITY STREET WALK

STUDIO AT THE UNIVERSITY OF MINNESOTA COLLEGE OF DESIGN, WITH STUDENT WORK BY JESSE BAULDRY MINNEAPOLIS, MINNESOTA

Program

Minneapolis's urban streets suffer from disrepair and lack of use. In the downtown core, urban street life is limited to small stretches along Nicollet Avenue, and only during the summer months. Current city initiatives have addressed the need for clearer transportation infrastructure and an improved pedestrian environment. However, Minneapolis has an extensive skyway system that provides unique connectivity and comfort to those familiar with its use, drawing pedestrians off the streets without offering visible access to the street. In their design project, Julie Snow and Matthew Kreilich focused their study on the sidewalks and "in-between" spaces of two urban streets in the downtown core, Nicollet Mall and Marquette Avenue, with possible interventions between these avenues.

Solution

City Street Walk offers three programmatically hybrid and varied interventions, on three different sites. A food stand/bus shelter, a skyway access point, and a newsstand/information station with interactive information and connections are located on the cross streets between Nicollet and Marquette. All three perform well year-round, embracing the challenges of Minnesota winters.

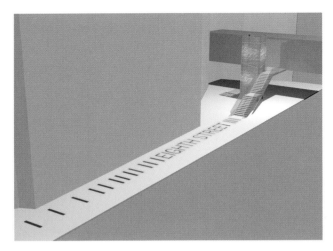

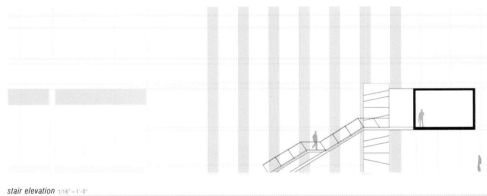

stair elevation 1/16" = 1'-0"

Operable skin enclosures used for the food stand and newsstand slide open to offer protection for patrons, or slide closed to protect the stand itself. This dynamic enclosure offers daily, seasonal, and operational options. Light and color animate all three installations. At the skyway access component, lights embedded in the sidewalk animate the street, direct users toward the skyway, and help locate the skyway user in the city. LED lighting and the use of heat-recovery systems to harvest warmth from adjoining buildings reduce the environmental impact of the proposed structures.

Each component is repeatable throughout the city, able to "plug" into the existing urban fabric at multiple locations while still maintaining an architecturally similar whole. Through the insertion of these new interventions, a broader, more cohesive system of private and public spaces along the avenues will be developed.

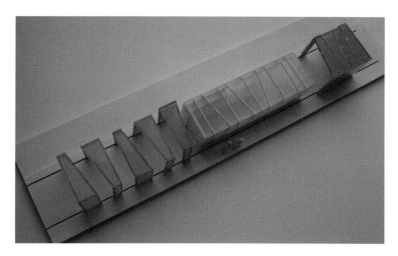

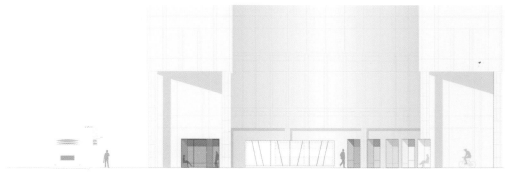

street elevation 1/8" = 1'-0"

→ **Reclaimed sidewalk materials
that define public theater**

**STUDIO LUZ:
UNION SQUARE
PERFORMANCE AREA**
SOMERVILLE, MASSACHUSETTS

Program

The city of Somerville, Massachusetts, held a competition to create a new performance area in Union Square, its oldest and largest commercial center, as a key component of its broader arts initiative, "ArtsUnion." Studio Luz's winning performance area project was commissioned to give Union Square a distinctive, creatively conceived space for public gatherings and performances.

Solution

Union Square Performance Area incorporates the architectural component of the street, literally reclaiming transitional granite curbing and redeploying it to form the performance area's edge. By creating an array of these self-similar members, an undulating surface is formed, allowing for seating, repose, or even a backdrop. The new form oscillates between landform, seating, and urban infrastructure. It also provides a large garden area for plantings. The performance area itself is defined by solar-powered illuminated bricks, absorbing solar energy by day and creating footlights by night.

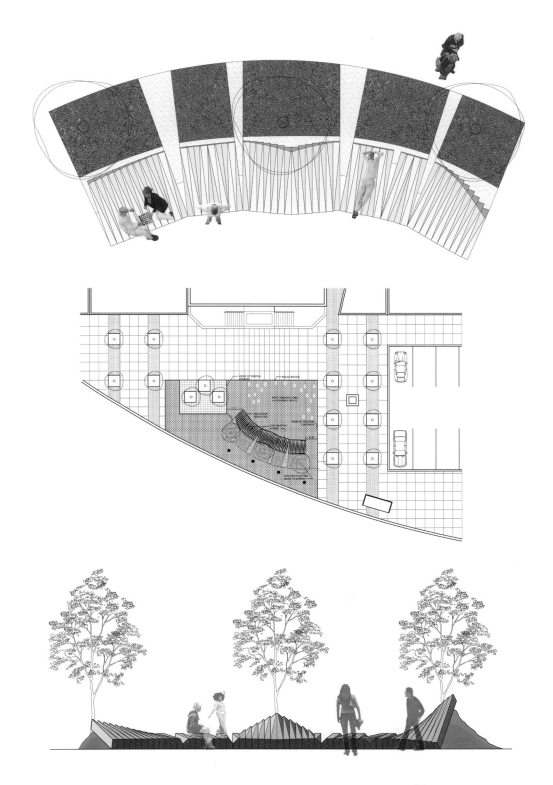

JAMES CORNER FIELD OPERATIONS AND DILLER SCOFIDIO + RENFRO: THE HIGH LINE

NEW YORK, NEW YORK

Program

The High Line is a one-and-a-half-mile-long public park built on an abandoned, elevated railroad stretching twenty-two city blocks, from the Meatpacking District to the Hudson Rail Yards, in Manhattan.

Solution

Inspired by the melancholic, "found" beauty of the railroad, where nature had reclaimed a once-vital piece of urban infrastructure, James Corner Field Operations and Diller Scofidio + Renfro designed the High Line to re-fit this industrial conveyance into a postindustrial instrument of leisure. By changing the rules of engagement between plant life and pedestrians, their strategy of "agri-tecture" combines organic and building materials into a blend of changing proportions that accommodates the wild, the cultivated, the intimate, and the social.

In stark contrast to the speed of nearby Hudson River Park, the singular linear experience of the new High Line landscape is marked by slowness, distraction, and an otherworldliness that preserves the strange, wild character of the High Line, without underestimating its intended use and popularity as a new public space. This notion underpins the overall strategy—the invention of a new paving and planting system that allows for varying ratios of hard to soft surface that transition from high-use areas (100 percent hard) to richly vegetated biotopes (100 percent soft), with a variety of experiential gradients in between.

The High Line's design respects the character of the railroad itself: its singularity and linearity, its straightforward pragmatism, and its relationship between wild plant life—meadows, thickets, vines, mosses, flowers—and industrial ballast, steel, and concrete. The architects' design solution was threefold. First, they created a paving system consisting of linear concrete planks with open joints and specially tapered edges and seams that permit intermingling of plant life with harder materials. Less a pathway and more a combed or furrowed landscape, this intermixing creates a textural effect of immersion, of strolling "within" rather than feeling distanced from. The selection and arrangement of grasses and plants further defines the park's wild, dynamic character, distinct from a typical manicured land-scape, and representative of the railroad's extreme conditions and shallow root-ing depth. The second strategy was to slow things down, to promote a sense of duration and of being in another place, where time seems less pressing. Long stairways, meandering pathways, and hidden niches encourage visitors to take their time. The third approach involved a careful sense of scale, minimizing the current tendency to make things bigger and obvious and seeking instead a more subtle gauge of the High Line's measure. The result is an episodic and varied sequence of public spaces and landscapes, set along a simple and consistent line—a line that cuts across some of the most remarkable elevated vistas of Manhattan and the Hudson River.

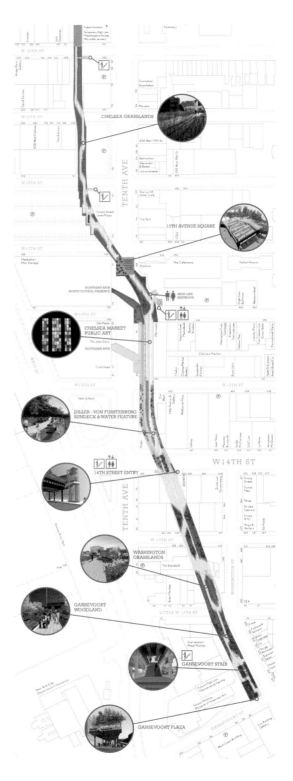

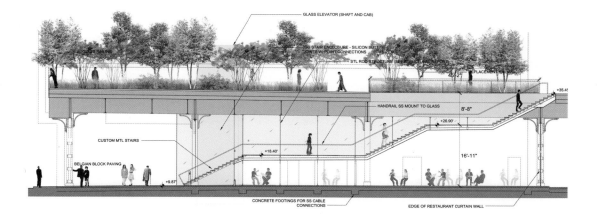

GLASS ELEVATOR (SHAFT AND CAB)

16U STAIR ENCLOSURE - SILICON BUTT
JOINTS W/ POINT CONNECTIONS

STL ROD STRUCTURE (SEE STRUCT WALL REPORT)

REPLACEMENT RAILING

GLASS RAILING

HANDRAIL SS MOUNT TO GLASS

8'-8"

CUSTOM MTL STAIRS

+26.90'

BELGIAN BLOCK PAVING

+18.40'

16'-11"

+9.87'

CONCRETE FOOTINGS FOR SS CABLE
CONNECTIONS

EDGE OF RESTAURANT CURTAIN WALL

AGRI-TECTURE: A FLEXIBLE, RESPONSIVE SYSTEM OF MATERIAL ORGANIZATION WHERE DIVERSE ECOLOGIES MAY GROW.

The striated surface transitions from high intensity areas (100% hard) to richly vegetated biotopes (100% soft), with a variety of experiential gradients in-between.

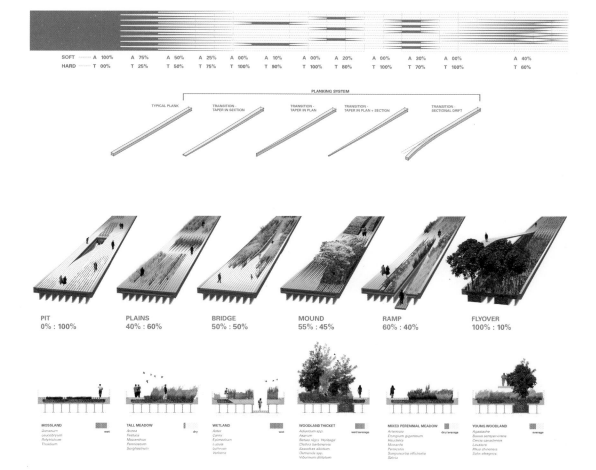

| | SOFT ---- A 100% | A 75% | A 50% | A 25% | A 00% | A 10% | A 00% | A 20% | A 00% | A 30% | A 00% | A 40% |
| | HARD ---- T 00% | T 25% | T 50% | T 75% | T 100% | T 90% | T 100% | T 80% | T 100% | T 70% | T 100% | T 60% |

PLANKING SYSTEM

TYPICAL PLANK | TRANSITION - TAPER IN SECTION | TRANSITION - TAPER IN PLAN | TRANSITION - TAPER IN PLAN + SECTION | TRANSITION - SECTIONAL DRIFT

| PIT | PLAINS | BRIDGE | MOUND | RAMP | FLYOVER |
| 0% : 100% | 40% : 60% | 50% : 50% | 55% : 45% | 60% : 40% | 100% : 10% |

MOSSLAND
Deranium
Leucobryum
Polytrichum
Thuidium
wet

TALL MEADOW
Avena
Festuca
Miscanthus
Pennisetum
Sorghastrum
dry

WETLAND
Aster
Carex
Epimedium
Luzula
Lythrum
Verbena
wet

WOODLAND THICKET
Adiantum spp.
Asarum
Betula nigra 'Heritage'
Clethra barbinervis
Sassafras albidum
Osmunda spp.
Viburnum dilatatum
wet/average

MIXED PERENNIAL MEADOW
Artemisia
Eryngium giganteum
Heuchera
Monarda
Persicaria
Sanguisorba officinalis
Salvia
dry/average

YOUNG WOODLAND
Agastache
Buxus sempervirens
Cercis canadensis
Lavatera
Rhus chinensis
Salix elegncs
average

INSIGHT

→ **A mysterious shadow message projected on an urban wall**

BUNCH DESIGN:
GREETING WALL
LOS ANGELES, CALIFORNIA

Program

A city is mostly made up of large, recognized elements, along with some "nonrecognized" parts and components—small phenomena, anomalous cases, ignorable parts, and weak connections. Although not major and mighty, these factors are the evidence, traces, and alibis of our everyday living environment. To place something new in the city often means to build new structures or add to/remove a large chunk of existing city, but the creation or discovery of something new could simply come from highlighting, exaggerating, remembering, or connecting things at hand, just like sticking a Post-it note on a page. Moments of attention and reexamination can be created through sleight of hand.

Solution

Bunch Design proposed a series of tactical interventions to highlight minor, hidden, sometimes-obvious-yet-overlooked "characters" in sites around Los Angeles, through random sampling and taxonomic fieldwork/observation. The project's intentions were less aimed at leaving behind objects of architecture, but more devoted to creating awareness, curiosity, and ways of (re)discovering what we already have.

Greeting Wall is a temporary message that appears on a blank urban wall every sunny afternoon. The words "Good Afternoon" are attached to a rooftop, and their shadow is cast onto the next building. In the mornings and evenings, the sun's angle prevents the greeting from being legible, or even visible, from the street.

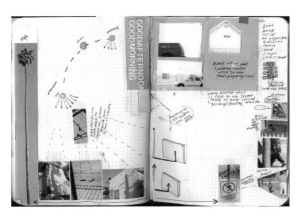

OWEN RICHARDS ARCHITECTS: MARK DION VIVARIUM

SEATTLE, WASHINGTON

Program

In the temperate rain forests of the Pacific Northwest, most nutrients must be bound in the vegetation, or else they would be leached away by the near-constant rain. When a toppled old-growth tree decays, it becomes a "nurse log," fostering diverse species of flora and fauna. These fallen giants become the foundation for the next generation of forest. Can this wonder of nature be moved to the city for enhanced human appreciation and access? What interventions are needed for a natural ecosystem to survive in an urban environment?

For centuries, museums have removed artifacts from their native settings, creating artificial environments to sustain the objects for human enlightenment. The Mark Dion Vivarium, which occupies a prominent corner of the Seattle Art Museum's Olympic Sculpture Park, explores the challenges of this grand tradition.

Solution

The vivarium, built by Owen Richards Architects in collaboration with artist Mark Dion, creates a life-support system for a fallen log, attempting to replicate the forest habitat within a new urban context. Blown over in a windstorm in 1991, the nurse log was discovered at the edge of an old-growth forest fifty miles from Seattle. The fifty-thousand-pound tree was removed with minimal damage to the surrounding ecosystem and relocated to its new urban site in 2006. A tapered greenhouse enclosure was then installed to follow the form of the nurse log.

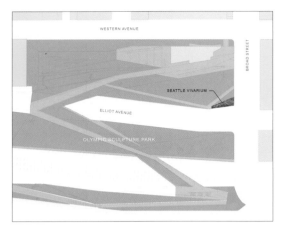

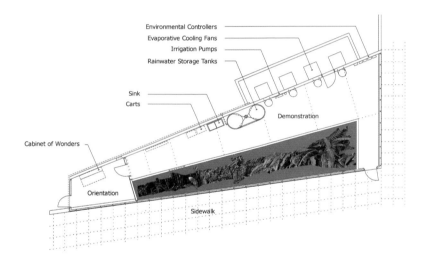

Environmental Controllers
Evaporative Cooling Fans
Irrigation Pumps
Rainwater Storage Tanks

Sink
Carts

Demonstration

Cabinet of Wonders

Orientation

Sidewalk

Horticulturalists from the University of Washington advised the Owen Richards Architects team on necessary sustainment systems. The vivarium's dense, green-glass roof maximizes photosynthesis by mimicking the color spectrum of the forest canopy. Large cisterns collect rainwater from the roof, feeding filtered irrigation and misting systems. Climate-control systems monitor temperature and humidity, operating vents and evaporative cooling fans that pump cool, humid air onto the tree.

Visitors observe life forms within the log using microscopes and magnifying glasses, supplied in a cabinet designed by the artist. Illustrations of log inhabitants decorate ceramic wall tiles that function as a field guide. The vivarium is a hybrid work of sculpture, architecture, environmental education, and horticulture.

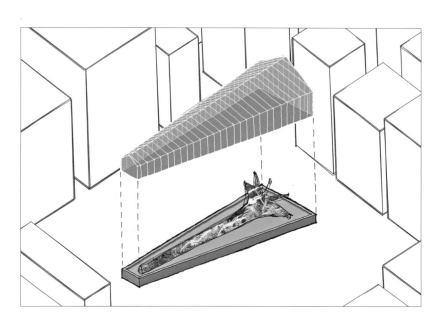

DILLER SCOFIDIO + RENFRO: FACSIMILE

SAN FRANCISCO, CALIFORNIA

Program

A tool of deception, Diller Scofidio+ Renfro (in collaboration with Ben Rubin of Ear Studio and Mark Hansen) created Facsimile as an installation at the Moscone Convention Center West in San Francisco in 2004.

Solution

Facsimile is a sixteen-foot-by-twenty-seven-foot video monitor, hanging from a traveling armature that glides along the periphery of the glass convention center. The one-hundred-foot-high armature moves very slowly along the outer contour of the building, guided on tracks at the parapet and soffit. Along with a camera mounted at a high elevation looking toward the city, a live video camera mounted back-to-back with the monitor points into the crowded prefunction space on the second level and transmits live feed to the street-facing monitor. The apparatus slowly scans the facade and broadcasts activity inside the lobby to the street. Fictional, prerecorded video programs that appear to be live (virtual views into a fictional office building, hotel, and lobby space during the natural course of day and night activities) are randomly substituted. While the live image naturally corresponds with the speed and direction of the scanning motion, the prerecorded programs are constructed to simulate the same speed. Thus, actual building occupants and interior spaces are confused with prerecorded impostors. As such, the apparatus could be seen as a scanning device, a magnifying lens, a periscope (with the high-elevation camera), and an instrument of deception. One round trip by the apparatus takes forty-five minutes.

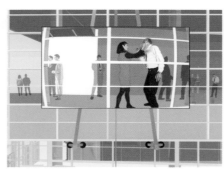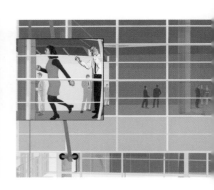

INSIGHT

ANTENNA DESIGN:
SIDEWALK SERIES
NEW YORK, NEW YORK

Program

Sidewalk Series—Shrink Bench, Hugging Tree, Exercise Stop, Escape Loft, Gum Sculpture, and Sidewalk Exchange—are proposed interventions for New York City sidewalks inspired by Antenna Design's observations of the city. The interventions, in the form of street furniture and fixtures, resonate with people's obscure yearnings and facilitate odd actions and temporary relationships between strangers. Their presence shifts the perception and experience of their various locations. The interactions and artifacts shape the impression of the city and become part of the urban experience.

Solution

Shrink Bench

New York is a stronghold of psychoanalysis, but many people simply just need to talk to someone. At the same time, there are people who love to listen to others' stories. The Shrink Bench invites anyone—possibly complete strangers—to be therapist or patient.

Hugging Tree

Despite being around millions of others in the city, sometimes people feel lonely, or feel regressive and wish they could cuddle in their parents' arms. The enhanced Hugging Trees respond to and communicate this need.

Exercise Stop

New Yorkers don't like to stop moving—
every second counts. Here, the traffic signal
is turned into an exercise "trainer" to make
use of waiting time. While participating in
this shared activity, people also have an
excuse to chat with each other.

Escape Loft

Sometimes people need to get away from
their daily chores, even if it's just for a few
minutes. Smoking has been banned in most
places in New York City, but on the Escape
Loft platforms, smokers can chill out and
socialize without bothering anyone or being
bothered by anyone.

Gum Sculpture

Gum Sculpture gives people a target to
deposit their used chewing gum on and
avoids the ugly gum stains on the floor.
It also exposes the tendencies of different
neighborhoods: "The sculpture in our
neighborhood has funny body parts."

Sidewalk Exchange

There are plenty of people on the sidewalk
who have something to sell, tell, or ask for.
The Sidewalk Exchange gives people a
proper setting to do this in a more civilized
manner and keeps the sidewalk neat.

REM KOOLHAAS AND CECIL BALMOND, WITH ARUP: SERPENTINE GALLERY PAVILION 2006
LONDON, ENGLAND

Program

Since 2000, the Serpentine Gallery has commissioned a different architect each year to design a temporary pavilion—to be used as a cafe by day and as a forum for learning, debate, and entertainment at night—on 2,100 square feet of lawn within the boundaries of the gallery. The project represents a rare opportunity for architects to create a more experimental structure in the United Kingdom, where none of those invited have ever built before. The gallery collaborates with the architect in the same way as it does with the artists who show at the Serpentine: by working to realize their vision for a project as they conceived it.

Solution

The Serpentine Gallery Pavilion 2006 was co-designed by Pritzker Prize–winning architect Rem Koolhaas and innovative structural designer Cecil Balmond. The pavilion consisted of three structural elements—a floor platform, a circular wall enclosure, and an inflatable floating canopy.

The pavilion's floor platform extended from the east side of the Serpentine Gallery across the lawn. The central area within the walled enclosure contained a number of mobile seating/table units, which could be arranged by visitors for eating, drinking, and more formal viewing.

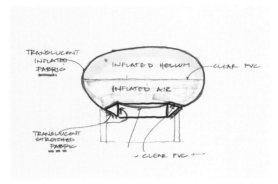

A circular enclosure composed of a series of five-meter-high translucent polycarbonate wall panels was built around the floor platform's perimeter. An inner circular wall constructed from the same material was set inside the outer wall, with a space of five feet between the two. Tensioned steel cables held the two walls in position. The pavilion's central space within the inner ring could be activated in a number of ways, depending on the time of day and public program, and could accommodate up to three hundred people.

The pavilion's ovoid, helium- and air-filled inflatable roof was the centerpiece of the design and could be raised and lowered to accommodate the activities within the structure. It provided protection from the weather—shade at the height of summer and rain and wind cover during autumn. The inflatable roof was sixty-five-feet high in its closed position, and could extend to a maximum height of seventy-eight feet when open. The roof was fabricated from translucent, PVC-coated polyester, and was illuminated from within at night.

The 2006 Serpentine Pavilion was designed to be defined by its events and activities. It was a space that facilitated the inclusion of individuals in communal dialogue and shared experience.

→ **A ticketing and viewing station for urban theater**

CHOI ROPIHA AND PERKINS EASTMAN: TKTS BOOTH

NEW YORK, NEW YORK

Program

The goal of this project was to provide an efficient, engaging, and consumer-friendly facility for TKTS—which sells discount tickets for Broadway plays and other performances throughout New York City—while also creating a new marker for Broadway, the Theater District, and all of the city's performing arts. Father Duffy Square—the location of the new TKTS Booth and the northern portion of the "bow tie" that is Times Square—has a dynamic spatial character generated by the intersecting of Broadway with the Manhattan street grid. It is a place of unrivalled urban intensity, driven by entertainment, information, and communication businesses.

The original brief focused on just replacing an already-existing TKTS booth, but the project's regenerative potential became clear early in the design process, and was expanded to become a more extensive inquiry about the relationships between TKTS, Father Duffy Square, and the broader context of Times Square and New York City.

Solution

The TKTS Booth's design stemmed from two instinctual responses: a resistance to placing a conventional building in the square, as this would undermine its spatial character; and an observation that, as one of the city's great gathering points, Times Square had nowhere for people to sit and enjoy the passing show.

118

INSIGHT

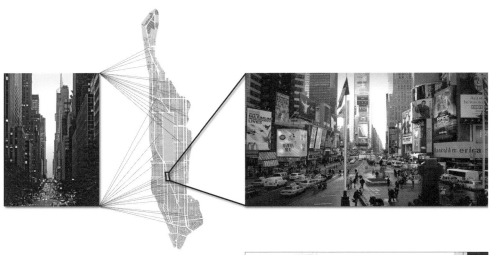

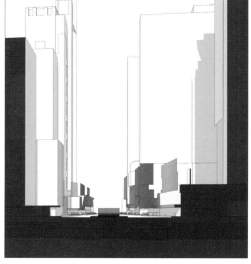

The booth has a series of red, luminescent steps rising from ground level that simultaneously act as a roof for the ticket booth—with twenty-four staff members and twelve ticket counters—and an inclined public space—capable of seating seven hundred people—where visitors and customers alike can pause to take in the "theater" of Times Square. Twenty-first-century technology gives the TKTS Booth further potency. Glass is its sole structural component, making the entire building translucent, while LED arrays beneath the steps create a powerful glow that makes the building part of the technological show of Times Square. Outside the booth, a deceptively simple plaza design organizes pedestrian movement while reinstating the prominence of the Father Duffy monument.

The multidimensional aspects of the project unite to amplify the presence of the booth and strengthen TKTS's position as a New York cultural institution, while the amalgamation of booth and plaza as a public venue has provided a new center for Times Square.

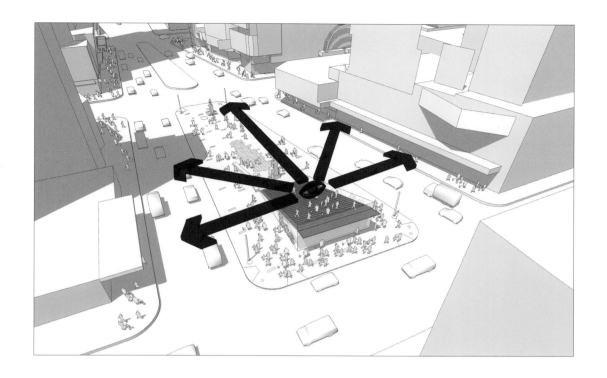

→ **Signage to confront social stereotyping**

```
DILLER SCOFIDIO + RENFRO:
HAVE YOU EVER
BEEN MISTAKEN FOR A...?
LILLE, FRANCE
```

Program

The deepening divide between French society and its unassimilated immigrant populations boiled over into civil unrest in the suburbs of Paris in 2005. Have You Ever Been Mistaken for a...?, made in collaboration with filmmaker Mira Nair, addresses the growing xenophobia in France and Western Europe in general.

Solution

Ten backlit screens evenly spaced along the main pedestrian street in Lille feature life-size fictional inhabitants of the city, apparently selected at random from the street. The images—shot in situ and displayed on lenticular screens—produce an uncanny sense of virtual transparency with physical depth and animation. Pedestrian viewers encounter each character sequentially. The characters perform ambiguous gestures that, in a climate of fear, could be construed as suspicious. The sequence of micromovies produces a sense of apprehension and, ultimately, self-reflection about our propensity to filter information and misread it.

KENNEDY & VIOLICH ARCHITECTURE: INTERIM BRIDGES PROTOTYPE
BOSTON, MASSACHUSETTS

Program

Constructed in a parking lot adjacent to Boston's Freedom Trail and Interstate 93, the one-hundred-foot-long Interim Bridges Prototype provided public viewing of an archaeological excavation and served as an outdoor classroom for Boston's public schools. Kennedy & Violich designed an exhibition, Temporary City, within the project that was open twenty-four hours a day.

The National Endowment for the Arts and the Massachusetts Cultural Council partially funded the Interim Bridges Prototype as a case study for the creation of new forms of urban public space during the demolition of Interstate 93 and its reconstruction underground, the so-called "Big Dig" project.

Solution

The Interim Bridges Prototype creates a new kind of public space where tourism and public education intersect with the disciplines of archaeology, engineering, and urban planning. The prototype connects the daily activities of commuters and the experiences of tourists on the Freedom Trail to the future location of the new roadway underground and the past life of the city. It engages the circumstances of the archaeological excavation and the reconstruction of the interstate as contemporary urban events that make visible the economic, political, and legal forces of property allotments, eminent domain, and zoning regulations that shape the physical form of the American city.

A standard wood-frame construction system was used to form a conical volume of space. This form expands the gap between the structure and the exterior skin to provide space for the exhibition and establishes a generosity of enclosure along the public walkway. Affordable materials and modes of assembly were necessary for the prototype, requiring a reconsideration of the idea and role of the detail in this provisional architecture. The detail resides in the material choice of a fiberglass envelope, and in an activation of the inherent properties of its surfaces and their capacity to reflect and radiate light.

The exhibition Temporary City presented historical documentation of the construction of the interstate in the 1950s, along with images of archaeological artifacts found each day at the excavation site. Where the structure of the elevated highway interrupts the prototype's envelope, it is reframed as an artifact of the exhibition.

INTERIM BRIDGES PROTOTYPE

STUDIO WORKS/B.A.S.E.:
GREEN COAT SURFACE
SHENZHEN, CHINA

Program

Green Coat Surface is part of City Disturbance, a series of projects proposed by architects Studio Works/B.A.S.E. for City Mobilization, the 2009 Shenzhen Hong Kong Bi-City Biennale. Green Coat Surface is intended to be a migratory piece, making its way around the world and through cities and landscapes. Upon arrival at each site, the configuration can be adjusted to take advantage of local conditions. Two potential sites for the Green Coat Surface are the Crystal Island and South Square, both in Shenzhen, China. Crystal Island is a major traffic island and South Square is a formal park at the center of the city, which is near the border between mainland China and Hong Kong.

Solution

The contemporary city can be simplified as a horizontal surface (often taken for granted and "untended") with objects (such as buildings) sitting on this surface. Green Coat Surface mimics these simplified features of the city, but takes corrective measures, provoking a questioning of the city's qualities. Green Coat Surface is an extension of Green Mao Jacket, a project by B.A.S.E. subgroup BASEline that referenced Mao's famous jacket and the impact he had on China. The Green Mao Jacket is a wearable coat made of the 100-percent-fireproof polypropylene mesh used in Chinese cities to wrap buildings under construction. Green Coat Surface takes this concept further into three forms: on the body, horizontal, and vertical.

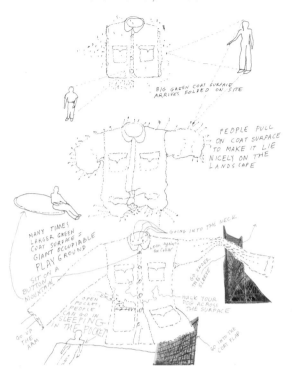

For the "on the body" form of Green Coat Surface, the Green Mao Jacket would be enlarged slightly to become more of a trench coat. Up to ten thousand coats would be distributed to visitors to City Mobilization. These people would act as "buzz marketers," provoking countless others to buy their own green coats, making them a kind of uniform for citizens.

Hanging from Shenzhen's Civic Center arch, the "vertical" version of Green Coat Surface would be long enough to reach to and spread out on the ground. City participants could then enter, leave, and re-enter the "inside" of Green Coat Surface. When inside the coat, participants would be within a civic space, albeit a soft one, and would be screened from the city itself.

The "horizontal" version of Green Coat Surface would straddle Crystal Island connecting Civic Square and South Square—not quite straight, and not quite on axis. The coat would be raised up onto bamboo structures, producing a wavy roof, constantly moving in the occasional breezes within Shenzhen. One would hope that this "provocateur" would stimulate the city residents into actions—musical, theatrical, commercial, and perhaps political. It would hopefully also stimulate them to occupy the coat (an oversized urban playground) by leaning on the collar, walking up the sleeve, sleeping in the pockets, sitting on a button mountain, and so on. At night, it would be lit and glow from within, so it could be inhabited twenty-four hours a day.

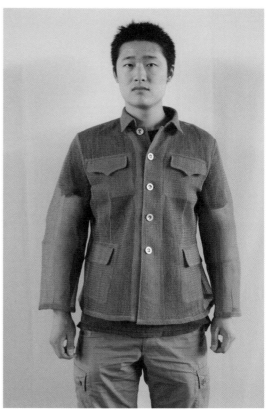

LOCAL PROJECTS:
IN PURSUIT OF FREEDOM
BROOKLYN, NEW YORK

Program

In Brooklyn, it's often quite easy to imagine the shadow of past events and figures on the borough's streets. However, for some neighborhoods years of neglect have erased all sense of history and place. In Pursuit of Freedom seeks to create a public connection to Brooklyn's rich history with abolitionism through neighborhood site-specific installations.

Solution

Life-sized images of individuals from various Brooklyn neighborhoods, sourced from the Weeksville Heritage Center and Brooklyn Historical Society archives, are featured on historical markers. Sited to a relevant historical location, these markers activate the space with a glimpse into the past life of each intersection. Moving past traditional site-making, which relies on austere plaques or stones, these sleek contemporary forms allow daytime visitors to gain a sense of the historic richness of these locations through photo-etched text and imagery forged onto stainless steel that fits soundly within the urban landscape. Adding to this experience, visitors can listen to era-inspired audio recordings via embedded headphone jacks, or by dialing or texting into a listed number located on the side of each marker.

At night, the markers subtly illuminate to maintain their presence, offering a connection to large, dynamic projections. Larger-than-life, these immersive images allow viewers to imagine the lives and activities that once existed in the surrounding environment. The projections amplify the presence of the site marker as well as the history that these markers represent. Carefully composited archival images are projected from streetlamps to nearby sidewalks, buildings, and walls via a permanent, rugged projection system. These images are designed to be viral—a media campaign within themselves, promoted by surprised onlookers taking photos of these street-level art installations, forwarding them to friends, and posting them online. Together, the projections, site markers, and audio recordings create story-places whose meaning is strengthened through invisible technology that propels accessible history forward into the twenty-first century.

INSIGHT

ADJAYE ASSOCIATES: SCLERA
LONDON, UNITED KINGDOM

Solution

When architect David Adjaye met with the American Hardwood Export Council and London Design Festival director Ben Evans to talk through the many potential timbers to use for Sclera, he chose tulipwood, also known as yellow poplar, because of its unique color and wide availability.

Often thought of as cheap or utilitarian, tulipwood is rather underappreciated. It comes from the tallest hardwood tree of North America, and grows abundantly throughout the eastern United States. Due to sustainably managed forests, its growth constantly exceeds its harvesting. Today it is primarily used by the furniture industry for interior joinery, kitchen cabinets, doors, and spindles. Sclera aimed to explore the possibilities of tulipwood, and hopefully increase its potential uses in the future.

Program

Sclera was a temporary pavilion created for the London Design Festival's Size+Matter program. It was installed in Festival Square at the Southbank Centre for one month. Festival Square is a busy, pedestrianized site that acts as a recreational destination in its own right while also providing access to popular venues within the Southbank Centre. Projects created for Size+Matter are intended to experiment with materials. Sclera expresses what one material (in this case, wood) is capable of and its behavior, while also altering existing perceptions of the material.

On first glance the design looks very simple, but the pavilion required a high level of craftsmanship, from the manufacturing of its precisely sized elements to their professional assembly. Additionally, the fabricator had to finish the project in under three months, from the original blueprints to manufacture and assembly. Made entirely of tulipwood, Sclera was an elliptical structure of approximately twenty-six by sixteen feet (eight by five meters), with two chambers inside. Visitors first entered a small, round chamber and experienced the pavilion's inner environment and its materiality. Then, passing through into the wider chamber, the experience gradually became about the view—a framing of the London Eye, echoing its circular forms, and the surrounding urban environment. The interior of the pavilion was characterized by an undulating pattern that appeared to be random but was based on a loose system of varying the lengths of the timber. The roof and sides had gaps in the slats, allowing light and wind to enter the pavilion, and at night Sclera was carefully lit, emitting a glow out into the square.

INSIGHT

SCHNEIDER STUDIO: MAKING TIME VISIBLE

BOSTON, MASSACHUSETTS

Program

"In a city, time becomes visible," according to historian Lewis Mumford. Yet in many places we've erased it. Downtown Boston has undergone—and continues to undergo—radical physical change. Scollay Square—at the site of one of the city's original seventeenth-century crossroads—was, by the early twentieth century, a crowded, tightly woven fabric of low buildings and narrow streets. Containing hotels, hot dog stands, liquor stores, and burlesque theaters, the square at that time was an infamous entertainment district. Urban renewal efforts in the 1960s bulldozed Scollay Square and transformed it into the monumental, vast Government Center that still occupies the site today. Twenty-two blocks were reshaped into six, giving the economically struggling city a much-needed new identity and international recognition. City Hall Plaza sits at the heart of Government Center, and urban designers, journalists, and the general public have decried the plaza's "windswept sea of bricks" ever since. The Trust for City Hall Plaza formed in 1995 to reimagine its future.

Solution

As Boston's citizens debated abstractly over the merits of a large civic plaza versus a collection of smaller buildings, Making Time Visible used Boston's current City Hall Plaza as the canvas for a nine-acre, life-size map of the same area a century ago. Guided by an 1895 Sanborn map, on August 27, 2002, two dozen volunteers drew 14,806 linear feet of chalk lines on top of City Hall Plaza's bricks. This temporary installation took advantage of the unique opportunity to illustrate what had been erased simultaneously with what had replaced it, and in doing so added context to the heated, often-misunderstood arguments over "pedestrian scale," "open space," and Boston's future urban public space, without a bias of what that future should be. Scollay Square historian David Kruh identified five sites of particular historic importance—where Alexander Graham Bell first heard the sounds of a human voice through a telephone, or where William Lloyd Garrison published *The Liberator*, for example—and the general public was invited to color in the chalk lines.

BERNARD TSCHUMI ARCHITECTS: GLASS VIDEO GALLERY
GRONINGEN, THE NETHERLANDS

Program

Commissioned by the city of Groningen as a temporary structure for a music and video festival, the Glass Video Gallery extends the public realm within a wooded traffic circle in the city's downtown, near the Groninger Museum. An inclined glass structure for viewing music videos and video-based installation art, the gallery is composed of a series of transparent, interlocking spaces. Seen as an extension of the tree-lined street in which it stands, the gallery allows the viewer to be viewed.

Solution

The Glass Video Gallery is a simple rectangular building made out of one material: glass. It responds to a contemporary architectural condition in which the appearance of permanence is increasingly challenged by the immaterial representation of abstract systems, in the form of television and electronic images. The city's invitation to design a special environment for viewing music videos also offered an opportunity to challenge preconceived ideas about spectatorship and privacy. Was the video gallery to be a static and enclosed black box, like the architectural type created for cinema? Would it be an extended living room, with exterior advertising billboards and neon lights? Or would it be a new "type" that brought what was previously a living room, bar, or lounge event out into the street?

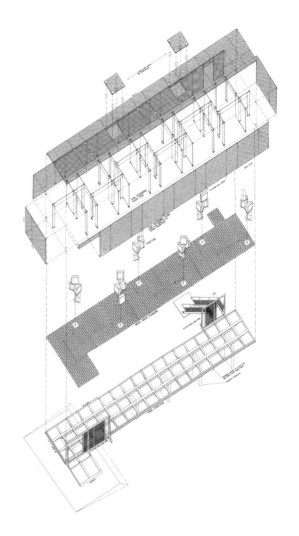

The video gallery explores the movement of the body as it travels through the exhibition space and enclosure, which is made entirely out of glass held by clips, including its vertical supports and horizontal beams. The resulting structure gives priority to the image. The monitors inside provide unstable facades, while the glass reflections create mirages, suggesting limitless space. At night, the space becomes an ensemble of mirrors and reflections, questioning what is real and what is virtual, and whether the envelope is an actual structure or an illusion. The Glass Video Gallery parallels urban space, inasmuch as both contain video objects, or tapes, that are on display, as well as methods for displaying them. These parallels extend to both the long monitor walls, viewed through "television dealership" storefronts on the street, and to the sex-video galleries of urban red-light districts.

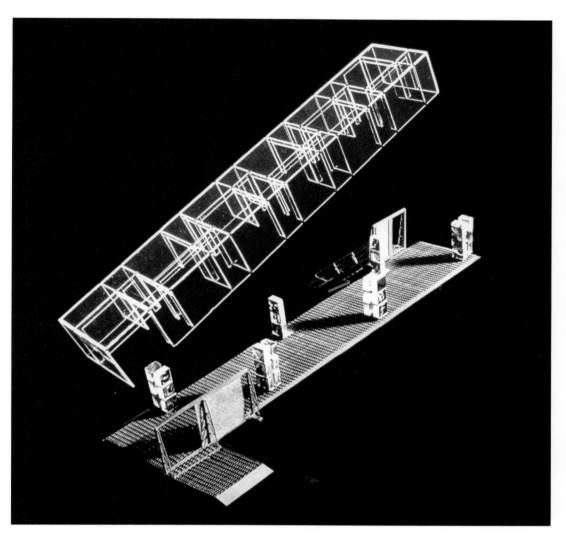

ERIC OWEN MOSS ARCHITECTS: THE ART TOWER

LOS ANGELES, CALIFORNIA

Program

The Art Tower is an information tower constructed in Los Angeles at the corner of Hayden Avenue and National Boulevard— the primary entry point into the redeveloped zone of Culver City. Conceptually, the tower has extroverted objectives. In reference to the growing community of new media companies, graphic designers, architects, and galleries, the tower provides a changing art display for local viewing. A variety of graphic content and data is offered on the five screens concerning upcoming events and current achievements of the tenants who occupy that part of the city. The Art Tower, located on a busy thoroughfare, also displays information for those driving through and anticipates the new passenger-railways system, the Expo Line light-rail, currently under construction.

Solution

All the buildings in the immediate area are governed by a fifty-six-foot height limit. The Art Tower is an important exception to the local height rule—it is seventy-two-feet high measured from grade, and will also include open-air, excavated, concrete seating and staging space at its base, which begins twelve feet below grade.

The tower consists of five circular steel rings, each approximately thirty feet in diameter. The rings are stacked at twelve-foot floor-to-floor intervals, and, as the height increases, are staggered in plan in order to establish proximity and viewing angles for various levels at various heights. The curving, conical projection screens are installed between each pair of staggered, horizontal circular steel planes. Digital projectors, twelve in all, hang behind these screens from the tower floors and rear-project onto the translucent acrylic screens. Inside the screens, steel decks are provided both for viewers to look out at the city and for the maintenance staff to service the projectors and screens.

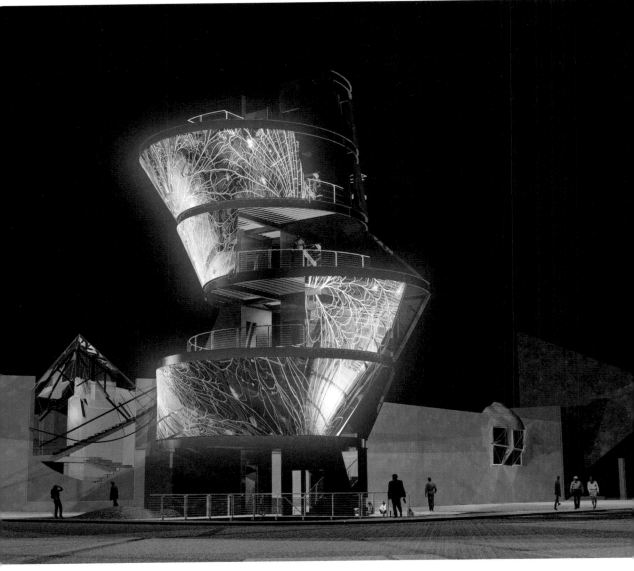

The Art Tower has a glazed elevator in an enclosed glass shaft, and an open-air stairway to the top. And, while the tower can be used as a viewing platform to overlook the city, its primary objective is to distribute art and other relevant content to the local and in-transit audiences passing by.

The tower is fabricated from standard structural steel sections—wide flange beams, columns, and channels—with panelized walls made of half-inch-thick steel plate. All the shapes and components were shop-fabricated and delivered to the site for erection. Because of earthquake design constraints, the tower is supported on a deep foundation of concrete piles, with a continuous-grade beam tying the piles together.

THE ART TOWER

DELIGHT

BALL-NOGUES STUDIO: MAXIMILIAN'S SCHELL
LOS ANGELES, CALIFORNIA

Program

Maximilian's Schell was created for Materials & Applications (M&A), a courtyard exhibition venue for experimental architecture and landscape that is open fourteen hours a day and is adjacent to a street busy with both pedestrian and automotive traffic. The project functioned as a shade structure, swirling overhead for the entire summer of 2005.

Solution

The interior of this immersive, experimental installation created a beckoning outdoor room for social interaction and contemplation by changing the space, color, and sound of the M&A courtyard gallery. During the day, as the sun passed overhead, the canopy cast colored, fractal light patterns onto the ground. When standing in the center, or "singularity," of the piece and gazing upward, the visitor could see only infinite sky. In the evening, when viewed from the exterior, the vortex glowed warmly.

Ball-Nogues Studio invested more than a year in developing Maximilian's Schell, going through several prototypes, though actual fabrication took only two weeks. The result was an installation that functioned not only as architecture and sculpture but as a made-to-order product, due to its unified manufacturing strategy. The designers achieved their aesthetic effects by manipulating Mylar reinforced with bundled nylon and Kevlar fibers with a computer numerical control (CNC) cutting machine. Simultaneously reflective and transparent, the amber-colored film had a UV-resistant, laminated, golden metallic finish.

The resulting project was neither a tent-type membrane nor a cable-net structure in the manner of Frei Otto, but a unique tensile matrix composed of 504 different instances of a parametric component, or "petal," each cut and labeled using the CNC system. Every petal connected to its neighbors at three points, using clear polycarbonate rivets to form the overall shape of a vortex. As though they were warped by the gravitational force of a black hole, the petals continually changed scale and proportion as they approached the singularity of the piece.

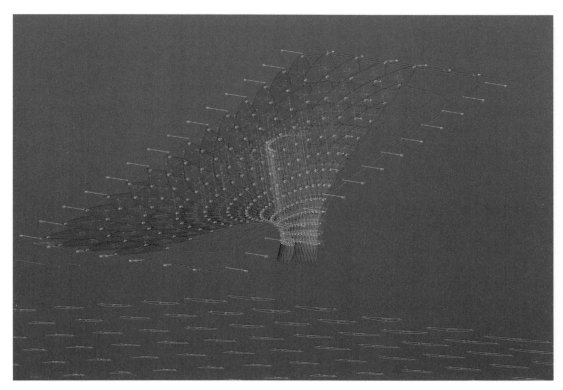

DELIGHT

GREYWORLD: BINS AND BENCHES
CAMBRIDGE, UNITED KINGDOM

Program

Bins and Benches was created for The Junction, an arts center in Cambridge, United Kingdom. During its redevelopment, the center commissioned an artwork for the new public square in front of its main building. Speaking about their inspiration for the project, Greyworld says, "It has always seemed to us that there are many objects placed in our public spaces, all with a certain dry function. What if we turned the tables, and we found ourselves in someone or something else's space? If the objects placed there by us actually lived and loved and frolicked? And in actual fact, it was us that were in their space?"

Solution

Five bins and four benches have been injected with a magical, life-giving serum, allowing them to break loose from their staid and fixed positions and roam around a public square in Cambridge. Travelling free and happy in their natural environment, they move and flock, drifting across the space. They frolic with the other species that inhabit their world, exploring their plaza and enjoying themselves.

Each bin or bench has its own personality and impulses—if it's raining, a bench may decide to park under a tree and wait for someone to sit on it, while on Wednesdays the bins line up, waiting to be emptied. Occasionally, they all burst into song, with the bins forming a baritone barbershop quintet and the benches a high soprano choir.

HÖWELER + YOON ARCHITECTURE: WHITE NOISE WHITE LIGHT

ATHENS, GREECE

Program

White Noise White Light was one of nine temporary, interactive urban installations commissioned and installed for the Athens 2004 Olympics. Part of a preplanned "Listen to Athens" route, the project inserted a luminous, interactive sound and landscape within the plaza entry to the Theater of Dionysus, below the Acropolis.

Solution

Höweler + Yoon Architecture embedded electronics into White Noise White Light to respond to individual bodies in a collective field condition. Visitors to the urban plaza encountered a grid of flexible, luminous stalks. Upon entering the open field, the visitors experienced "washes" of white light and white noise, triggered by their movements.

White Noise White Light consisted of a field of fiber-optic stalks, a raised deck, and four hundred custom-designed electronics modules. Each module contained a passive-infrared sensor and microprocessor, which modulated the brightness of LEDs at the tips of the fiber-optic stalks as well as the volume of a sound file played through the speakers. The field's distributed responsiveness allowed each stalk to individually gauge the degree of bodily presence so that when people's motions ceased, each microprocessor smoothly lowered the light of each stalk and faded the white noise to silence. Collectively, the units responded to the movement of pedestrians with an afterglow effect. A flickering wake of white light and white noise trailed and traced each visitor's path.

Depending on the time of day, number of people, and trajectories of movement, White Noise White Light constantly recorded the cumulative interaction of the public. Visitors attempted to decode the installation's responsive parameters by experimenting with their bodies in space: running, dodging, stamping, and tiptoeing. The field became an unpredictable aggregation of movement, light, and sound—a site of play within the city. Essential to the project was the idea that individuals could affect the field. Their actions produced new behaviors and ripple effects of reactions from the environment and the people around them.

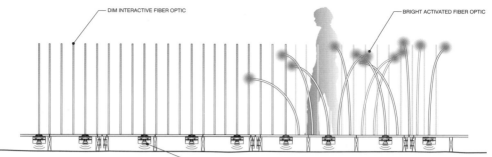

DIM INTERACTIVE FIBER OPTIC

BRIGHT ACTIVATED FIBER OPTIC

SPEAKER EMITTING WHITE NOISE

CENTERBROOK ARCHITECTS AND PLANNERS: THREAD CITY CROSSING

WINDHAM, CONNECTICUT

Program

In the nineteenth century, Windham, Connecticut, was called "Thread City" because of its nearly one million square feet of thread factories, many powered by the Willimantic River. The town straddles the river, and a new bridge was needed to connect the borough's suburbs to its historic commercial center. Engineers hired by the Connecticut Department of Transportation (DOT) originally designed a standard interstate bridge for the site. Local people were offended by this design and demanded that the bridge be sensitive to its historic setting, so the city approached Centerbrook Architects and Planners for suggestions on how to add character to this utilitarian bridge.

Solution

Centerbrook began their work by meeting with the local bridge design committee, which included the mayor, representatives of the local planning agencies, the town historian, and concerned citizens. As the project progressed, Centerbrook included the committee in the design process. Citizen involvement enriched the final design and was key to building public support for the new bridge plan.

Thread City Crossing now serves as a gateway to the town and the historic district, incorporating symbols of Windham's history and industry. Giant concrete spools of thread sit above each of the bridge abutments, and twelve-foot-tall bronze frogs enliven the spools at each end of the bridge. The spools recall Windham's history as a major thread producer. The frogs were suggested by David Phillips, a member of the bridge design committee and a professor at Eastern Connecticut State University, based on the legend of the Windham Frogs. Windham gained renown one night in June of 1754, during the French and Indian War, when the townspeople were awakened by a tremendous noise. Expecting an attack and fearing for their lives, they ran from their homes to hide in the woods. The noise turned out to be bullfrogs fighting for the last drops of water in a dried-up millpond.

Centerbrook contacted sculptor Leo Jensen to create frogs for the bridge that were beautiful and a bit sassy. Local citizens then raised money to have Jensen make a quarter-scale wood model of a frog on a spool to publicize the design and help raise money for the full-size frogs. After intensive lobbying from the community, the DOT paid for the frog sculptures out of the construction budget.

STOSS LANDSCAPE URBANISM: SAFE ZONE
GRAND MÉTIS, QUEBEC, CANADA

Program

Safe Zone was a temporary, 3,400-square-foot garden installation commissioned for the 2006 International Garden Festival, held at Jardins de Métis/Reford Gardens in northeast Quebec. The site selected for this installation was rectangular, with the shorter dimension on the greater garden festival path. The existing conditions were approximately half wooded, half cleared.

Solution

The garden used off-the-shelf safety products (poured-in-place rubber, safety tiles, goal post bumpers) turned or stretched to new ends. Safe Zone established a topography of code and regulation, manufacturing three-dimensional garden conditions (hillocks and valleys). The garden was a contemporary reinterpretation of the classic pleasure garden: playful, tactile, sensual, engaging, uncertain, insidious, perhaps even risky.

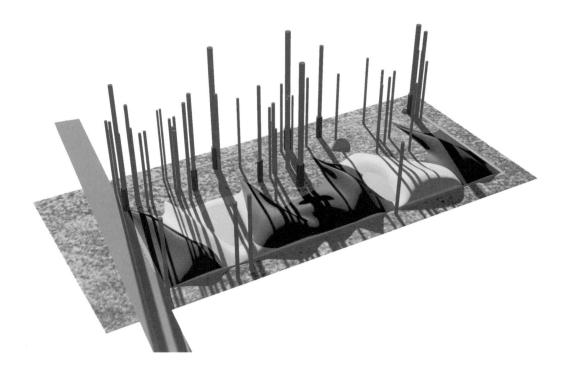

The design innovatively employed commercial products designed for dangerous situations in everyday landscapes (subway platforms, sidewalks, playgrounds, sports fields), coerced into a provocative public space. The garden did so in response to government safety codes and regulations, which typically alienate people in the public realm. Here, those same codes, and the materials used to meet them, were turned around, opening up possibilities for free, uninhibited movement and exploration. Safe Zone was meant to encourage people's curiosity and sense of experimentation, causing them to shed preconceptions and self-consciousness in an encounter with the unknown.

The garden's main material, poured-in-place rubber, was especially unique. Often used as a flat surface beneath playground structures to cushion falls, the rubber is fantastically squishy. For Safe Zone, Stoss Landscape Urbanism pushed this material property, installing it thinner at the hillocks' crests and thicker at their bases, varying its thickness to amplify its ability to destabilize. Changes in resistance to one's body weight could actually induce one to fall—into a pit, onto another visitor— or encourage one to burrow or bounce.

The garden established a new sustainable aesthetic: while it was clearly synthetic, 80 percent of the materials used in it were either recycled or salvaged from sneaker soles, old tires, and discarded tiles. The surface was also permeable, allowing water to penetrate to irrigate tree roots and recharge the water table.

BARNABY EVANS: WATERFIRE
PROVIDENCE, RHODE ISLAND

Program

Downtown Providence, Rhode Island— once a thriving community—had seen most of its industries leave over the past one hundred years, and was empty and dangerous on nights and weekends. In the early 1990s, the city opened up a long-covered river to form a mile of park through downtown that, despite excellent design, extensive pedestrian amenities, and thoughtful engagement with history, remained largely underused and failed to stimulate new construction in the area. WaterFire was created in 1994 to reinforce this initial effort and bring economic activity to Providence. A deeper mission was to inspire the city's residents to realize its potential and create a symbol for its prosperous future and renaissance.

Solution

Artist Barnaby Evans designed WaterFire as a public artwork that modifies the experience of public space and makes the urban environment the actual canvas of the work of art. WaterFire is a series of nearly one hundred bonfires lining the surface of Providence's three rivers. It is a combination of light and fire, public ritual, subtle design, crowd psychology, community engagement, unusual recorded music, and live performances that forge a new vision for the downtown. Relying on spectacle and surprise to transform the visitor's expectation of the urban experience, WaterFire is a free, pedestrian-based exploration of the downtown district. It combines a wide variety of installations and performances with a core ritual of redemption, with the light of its bonfires representing the renewal of life downtown. WaterFire, now a yearly festival, has attracted more than ten million visitors to downtown Providence, transformed the city into a destination, and sparked a broad reevaluation of the city and its future.

GREYWORLD: RAILINGS

LONDON, UNITED KINGDOM
PARIS, FRANCE

Program

Railings was installed in 1997 without permission in public spaces around Paris and London by tuning the preexisting metal railings on the sites. Some examples remain, especially in the centers of both cities. According to Greyworld, "Public art is a flawed term. What is public about the bronze man on a horse, or the highly polished rock so beloved of town planners?" They set out to create artworks that would reappropriate the elements of urban space and allow some kind of creative expression in areas where usually there is none.

Solution

Railings plays on the simple pleasure of picking up a stick and running it along a set of railings to make a lovely "clack-clack-clack" sound. We loved doing this as children, but often forget about it as adults. Greyworld chose railings in small green spaces, side alleys, and other liminal locations, then tuned the railings using one of three methods so that when you run a stick along them, they play "The Girl from Ipanema."

There was no plaque to let passers-by know about the intervention. The architects hoped, instead, that people might just pick up a stick and have a play anyway—perhaps the railings would play a tune, perhaps not.

IN COLLABORATION:
GROUND, HÖWELER + YOON ARCHITECTURE, LINOLDHAM OFFICE, MERGE ARCHITECTS, MOS, SSD, STUDIO LUZ, UNI, UTILE INC., AND OVER,UNDER
PARTI WALL, HANGING GREEN
BOSTON, MASSACHUSETTS

Program

The shifting development patterns of Boston's evolving urban landscape have created conditions where urban infill lots sit empty. Bare parti walls (short for partition wall, or the lot-line wall) are symptomatic of this uneven development. The vacancy of these urban lots and their provisional uses, typically consisting of grade parking, made them an ideal test site for Parti Wall, Hanging Green—a vertical green wall created by a group of young Boston-area architecture firms.

Solution

Parti Wall, Hanging Green consists of panels of live vegetation suspended from cables and forming an overall abstract pattern. It aims to transform the character and texture of the urban environment—providing visual relief, color, and texture—as well as to bring a range of ecological benefits—including insulation, sound absorption, reduction of storm water runoff, and mitigation of the heat-island effect.

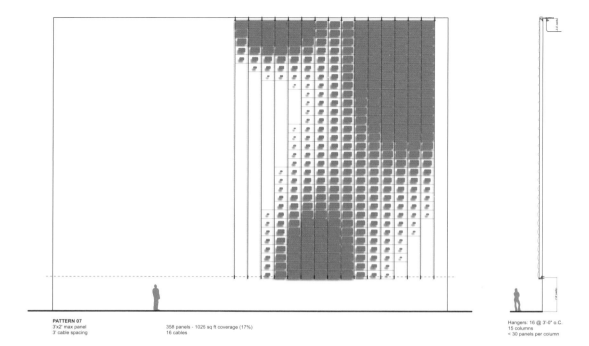

PATTERN 07
3'x2' max panel
3' cable spacing

358 panels - 1025 sq ft coverage (17%)
16 cables

Hangers: 16 @ 3'-0" o.c.
15 columns
< 30 panels per column

The project is a prototype, in the sense that it proposes a system of components capable of being deployed to sites across the city. After testing several varieties of grasses and groundcovers, the architects selected sedum for its visual properties as well as its resilience. The panelized nature of the installation allows for the easy removal of individual modules and the substitution of other varieties. The hope is that the prototype will demonstrate the feasibility of vertical landscaping, as well as promote a larger discussion about urban ecologies, microclimates, and vegetal effects.

JANET ECHELMAN:
HER SECRET IS PATIENCE
PHOENIX, ARIZONA

Program

Downtown Phoenix has never had a public gathering space where residents would spend time by choice. The new, two-city-block Civic Space Park is intended to create an enticing public space in order to foster a sense of community. Janet Echelman's sculpture *Her Secret is Patience* is suspended in the center of the park and acts as an iconic landmark of a new cultural identity for the city. The sculpture creates a sense distinct yet equally compelling environments during both day and night to visually attract people to the downtown civic areas.

Solution

The 145-foot-tall sculpture is monumental, yet also soft and flexible, with its semi-translucent weave. Its lightness allows it to be animated by "wind choreography," which engages people emotionally and kinesthetically, drawing many viewers to lie down on the grass underneath it for extended periods of time. The elevated location of *Her Secret is Patience* pulls the gaze up to the sky and optimizes a relatively small footprint for a downtown park by allowing the same area to be both recreational and iconic sculpture at the same time. Local curator Marilu Knode says that Phoenix "finally has a heart."

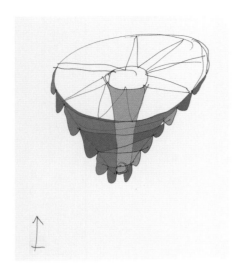

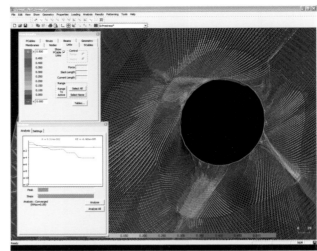

The sculpture's multilayered form was created with a combination of hand-baited and machine-loomed knotting, and is the result of a collaborative effort with an international team of award-winning engineers. During the day, the high-tenacity, polyester-net sculpture projects "shadow drawings" onto the ground, inspired by Phoenix's cloud shadows. The piece appears delicate and diaphanous, a unique quality for outdoor sculpture, and incorporates the surrounding landscape. *Her Secret is Patience*'s visual form makes reference to local desert flora (such as night-blooming cacti), Phoenix's distinctive monsoon cloud formations, and the city's geologic history (the local fossil record shows evidence that this site was once an ocean filled with marine life). At night, the illumination program changes color gradually through the seasons, enhancing without overpowering the richness of the net's integrally colored fibers. The lighting design also changes what portion of the sculpture is illuminated, leaving parts obscured in mystery.

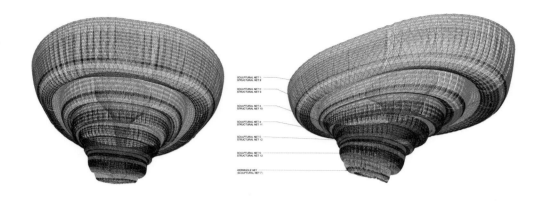

SCULPTURAL NET 1 / STRUCTURAL NET 8
SCULPTURAL NET 2 / STRUCTURAL NET 9
SCULPTURAL NET 3 / STRUCTURAL NET 10
SCULPTURAL NET 4 / STRUCTURAL NET 11
SCULPTURAL NET 5 / STRUCTURAL NET 12
SCULPTURAL NET 6 / STRUCTURAL NET 13
WORMHOLE NET (SCULPTURAL NET 7)

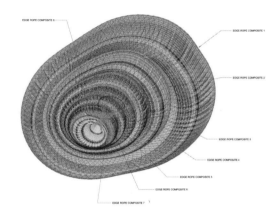

EDGE ROPE COMPOSITE 8
EDGE ROPE COMPOSITE 1
EDGE ROPE COMPOSITE 2
EDGE ROPE COMPOSITE 3
EDGE ROPE COMPOSITE 4
EDGE ROPE COMPOSITE 5
EDGE ROPE COMPOSITE 6
EDGE ROPE COMPOSITE 7

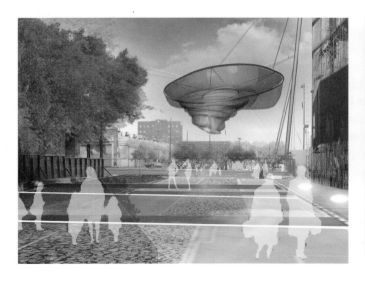

nARCHITECTS: CANOPY

LONG ISLAND CITY, NEW YORK

Program

Canopy was a temporary structure created by nArchitects for the courtyard of the P.S.1 Contemporary Art Center in Long Island City, New York. The courtyard space hosts weekly Warm Up music parties, which attract eight thousand revelers every Saturday in the summer.

Solution

The word canopy refers to both a rooflike structure and the uppermost region of a forest. The architects developed the idea of a "deep landscape" to stitch together the limits of the existing site (ground, concrete walls, sky) with one material. Canopy was built with green bamboo and existed for five months. During this time, it was host to more than one hundred thousand visitors and underwent a slow transformation as the freshly cut green bamboo turned from green to tan, allowing visitors to experience the effects of time in a direct and tactile way.

Canopy relied on a singular tectonic system for shade, structure, and atmosphere. Pinches in the undulating lattice produced a range of shadow densities and patterns across the courtyard. Dips in the canopy defined rooms open to the sky, each with a distinct climatic environment for different modes of lounging: a Pool Pad incorporated a large wading pool; a Fog Pad was surrounded by nozzles that spread a halo of cool mist on revelers; the Rainforest featured a sound environment and misters that provided intermittent rain showers and randomly soaked the crowd; and a Sand Hump's sandy cove maximized exposure to either sun or shade.

ARC PROFILES

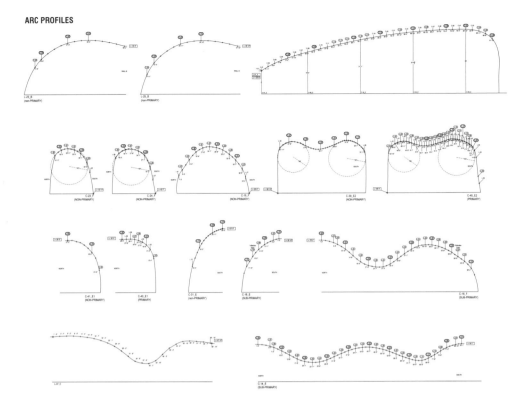

The project's challenge resided in the physical translation of a geometrically precise structure using a natural material with inherently variable characteristics. The architects digitally modeled each arc in Canopy in three dimensions, and then exported these into two-dimensional elevation drawings, with the arc's exact length and intersection points indicated. The type, general shape, and critical radius of an arc dictated its pole selection, orientation, and splicing method. With their team of architecture students and recent graduates, nArchitects then spent six weeks on-site testing each arc type to determine the maximum span, minimum bending radii, and overlap dimensions before building the structure itself over a period of seven weeks. The project used thirty-thousand feet of flexible, freshly cut green *Phyllostachys aurea* bamboo from Georgia, spliced and bound together with thirty-seven-thousand feet of stainless-steel wire. The final canopy lattice acted as a multidirectional structural network of more than three hundred individual arcs whose shapes were precisely translated from the digital model.

At the end of the summer, nArchitects sold the bamboo as raw material to the studio of artist Matthew Barney for the construction of scaffolding in a film set. Everyone assumed that the bamboo would have lost its elasticity after being effectively molded into shape for so long, so it was a surprise when the bamboo immediately sprang back to being straight as soon as it was cut loose.

CHO BENN HOLBACK + ASSOCIATES: THE HUGHES FAMILY OUTDOOR THEATER
BALTIMORE, MARYLAND

Program

The American Visionary Art Museum (AVAM) is dedicated to the study, collection, preservation, and exhibition of artworks created by self-taught artists, and to using such art to explore and expand the definition of a worthwhile life.

The Rouse Visionary Center on AVAM's campus, designed by Cho Benn Holback + Associates, is dedicated to the goals of the late urban visionary Jim Rouse. The Center for Visionary Thought, housed within this building, promotes low-cost, grassroots solutions to improving urban life while furthering Rouse's belief that "cities are meant to be gardens in which to grow beautiful people." The museum wanted to embody this notion by extending beyond its doors, embracing the community and celebrating urban life and art.

Solution

AVAM began its "Flicks from the Hill" outdoor family-film series in the spring of 2005. Inspired by the popularity of Little Italy's outdoor film series, AVAM took great advantage of the adjacent three-tiered, grassy green slope of Federal Hill Park—using it as a natural outdoor amphitheater, capable of easily seating more than one thousand people with clear visual and audio access. Federal Hill is an ideal perch to gather in warm weather to watch movies under the stars, and the city enthusiastically granted permission for this usage. Movies themed around the current museum exhibition are shown on Thursdays throughout the summer.

AVAM board member Patrick Hughes established the Hughes Family Outdoor Theater with initial funds for the purchase and installation of a giant, thirty-two-foot outdoor movie screen on the rear wall of the Rouse Visionary Center, as well as the delightful twelve-foot-tall Golden Hand, a sculpture by Adam Kurtzman that projects from above the screen, giving the illusion of a "divine hand" supporting the public movie screenings.

STUDIO D'ARC ARCHITECTS WITH JEREMY BOYLE: V365/24/7

PITTSBURGH, PENNSYLVANIA

Program

V365/24/7 is a collaborative project designed by Studio d'ARC Architects and artist Jeremy Boyle for the Pittsburgh Downtown Partnership's (PDP) public art competition for Strawberry Way, a much-used, three-block-long downtown pedestrian thoroughfare. The V365/24/7 proposal responded to the found conditions along Strawberry Way with a unique understanding of light, along with the twin goals of being self-sustainable and easily demountable. The primary elements that define the alley are natural light, vertical space, and the relationship to the horizontal ground plane of the pedestrian passage, especially on a block bounded by the city's AT&T Building, Reed Smith Building, and First Lutheran Church.

Solution

Observing the way light and shadow played on the AT&T Building from First Lutheran's spire, the design team realized the relationship of sunlight and shadow was quite different for the pedestrian throughout the year. From this, they developed the idea of collecting sunlight from this vertical space, far from the reach of the pedestrians below, and to transform this energy into a new form and experience in Strawberry Way. Location, the time of day, and the time of season would inform and accompany the passersby on their daily commutes.

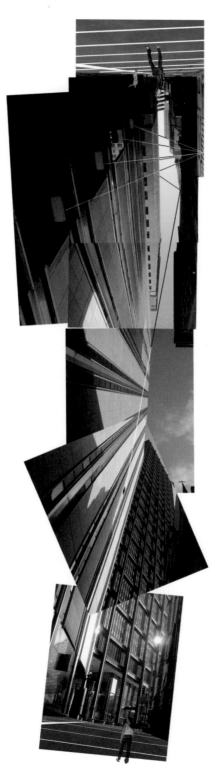

Solar Study on the Vertical Surface of the AT&T building (South Face located on Strawberry Way)

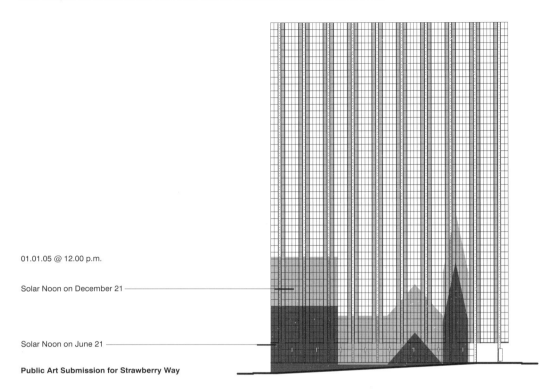

01.01.05 @ 12.00 p.m.

Solar Noon on December 21 ————————————

Solar Noon on June 21 ————————————

Public Art Submission for Strawberry Way

Using a solar panel on the AT&T Building, collected light is transformed into energy, which then powers a computer-generated algorithm that loosely translates the well-known composition by Antonio Vivaldi, *The Four Seasons*. This music was selected for its direct connection to time and season, as well as for its familiarity. The audio signal travels to four speakers positioned along Strawberry Way. The music shifts slowly throughout the day and, like the Vivaldi piece from which it is based, evolves with the changing seasons, giving a unique musical description to both the time of day and time of year in a 365-day composition.

Shadow Studies of Street Context

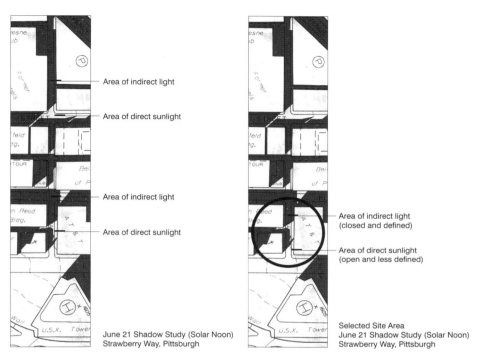

Area of indirect light

Area of direct sunlight

Area of indirect light

Area of direct sunlight

June 21 Shadow Study (Solar Noon)
Strawberry Way, Pittsburgh

Area of indirect light
(closed and defined)

Area of direct sunlight
(open and less defined)

Selected Site Area
June 21 Shadow Study (Solar Noon)
Strawberry Way, Pittsburgh

Public Art Submission for Strawberry Way

Conceptual Sketches (making something happen in the shadows)

Light as a natural
power source

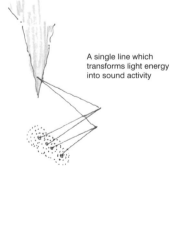

A single line which
transforms light energy
into sound activity

Public Art Submission for Strawberry Way

MARK RYAN STUDIO WITH MAYME KRATZ: TRUENORTH

TEMPE, ARIZONA

Program

Thought of conceptually as a campfire at the edge of the water, trueNorth sits at the northern periphery of downtown Tempe, Arizona, as part of the Tempe Center for the Arts, immediately adjacent to the southwestern bank of Tempe Town Lake.

Solution

TrueNorth functions primarily as a hearth—a gathering place and a focus point both for the art center itself and the surrounding community. It provides seating, including wheelchair accessibility, and accommodates drainage and circulation concerns, yet it also attempts to transcend the necessary, utilitarian aspects of its program in order to form a place of meaningful connection. The work has an appearance from afar that is intentionally distinct from the personal, more intimate reading when confronted up close. The project is simultaneously inward-looking and focused out beyond its constructed boundaries.

Rooted in the long history of this particular place, trueNorth was inspired by an American Indian legend of the Great Spirit. Passed down through generations of several tribes, the story tells of the Great Spirit assigning guardianship of the earth, wind, fire, and water to different races of people and assigning them a direction. To the north, the Great Spirit gave fire.

From the geometric center of the art center's semicircular plan, a line was struck on the true north alignment. This axis emanates outward from the project and extends across the water, through the foothills of the Papago Buttes to Camelback Mountain and beyond. Lining up the flames of two hearths, viewed through a strategically placed aperture, connects the individual to this greater perspective.

Early walks on the site revealed something interesting, a bit of unexpected magic. The ground seemed to sparkle. A photograph of this phenomenon, thought of as a site-specific constellation, was mapped on the surface of trueNorth's black concrete plinth and determined the particular placement of 120 individually cast resin rods. Suspended within each resin rod is some special aspect of the project: sketches from the process, correspondence, screenplays, sheet music, poetry, or natural objects collected from the site.

ROBERTO ROVIRA AND AZIMUTH STUDIO: I-880 GATEWAY

OAKLAND, CALIFORNIA

Program

Interstate 880 is an undeniable component of Oakland's vehicular and pedestrian landscape. The massive highway displaces urban fabric and severs the continuity between the city's revitalized waterfront and its downtown. Even though the areas below the highway's overpass experience a large amount of pedestrian traffic, they were an undeniable product of car culture. A forest of columns, the thick concrete slab above, the oversize turning radius of the ramps, and the soot collected on all surfaces were all indicative of a place designed almost exclusively for cars. A competition brief called for a gateway that would transform this otherwise unforgiving environment.

Solution

I-880 Gateway, the winning competition entry, proposed an experiential pedestrian and vehicular gateway that would respond to—and not conceal—the innate qualities of this critical urban threshold. The proposal embraced materials that were "natural" to the context of the highway: guardrails, recycled car tires, LED lights, red safety paint. The highway's material vocabulary became an essential part of a design that transformed the space while simultaneously embracing its inherent identity. The common reading of building materials used almost exclusively within the domain of vehicular infrastructure was countered by their unconventional application, as elements that weave around brightly painted columns and help dissolve the overpass's imposing scale.

Although not all the proposed elements were employed (such as an undulating, recycled rubber sidewalk flanking the road and pulsating LED lights that would register the movement of cars above the overpass), sculptural walls made of highway guardrail material and brightly painted and illuminated red columns provide a language that addresses the urban problem of interstitial spaces that were designed for vehicles but that inevitably encroach on the pedestrian experience of a city.

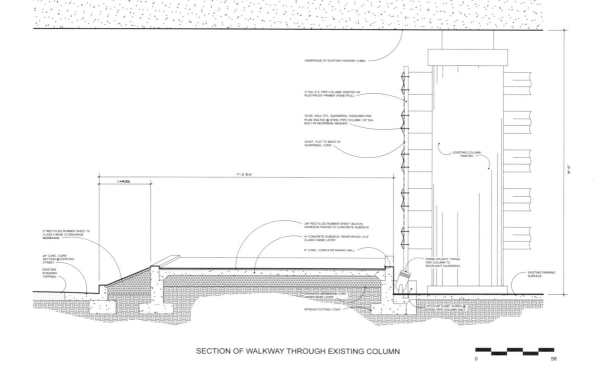

SECTION OF WALKWAY THROUGH EXISTING COLUMN

0   5ft

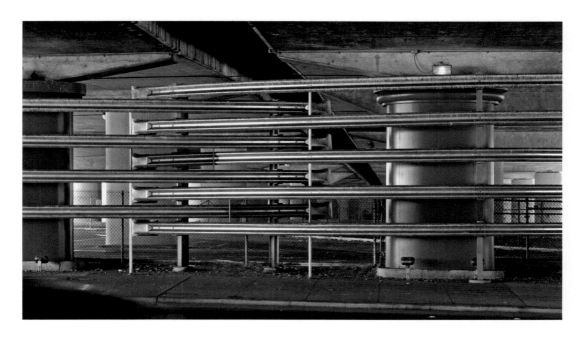

→ **Recreational pavilions and utilitarian amenities**

```
┌─────────────────────────────┐
│   SHoP ARCHITECTS:          │
│   MITCHELL PARK             │
│   GREENPORT, NEW YORK       │
└─────────────────────────────┘
```

Solution

The five-acre site spans from the last Long Island Rail Road station on the North Fork and the Shelter Island ferry terminal at the west, to a public marina and commercial zone to the east. The spaces between these destinations are linked by a hardwood boardwalk and a delineated network of bluestone and stabilized gravel paths. The park's collection of architectural programs radiates from a multi-use plaza situated at the visual center of the site.

The plaza supports an amphitheater and an open-air, seasonal ice rink that turns into a mist garden during the warm summer months. The mist garden is flanked by a contemporary house for a vintage carousel, shade arbors, a mechanical building, and a camera obscura. The palette of building claddings (ipe, cedar, and zinc) responds to the coastal environs, as they develop a patina over time.

Program

Mitchell Park is located in Greenport, a historic seaport at the eastern edge of Long Island's North Fork. Its proximity to farmland and a sheltered deep harbor supported commercial industries and recreational activities throughout its long history. Founded in 1838, Greenport's past is marked with significant episodes of change. In 1996, the town embarked on a nine-year campaign to revitalize its public, commercial, and recreational infrastructure. Mitchell Park is the nucleus of this program, which evolved from the acquisition of private land parcels with the assistance of state and local agencies. The project's intent was to activate and build upon existing transportation and commercial infrastructure through a mesh of recreational pavilions and utilitarian amenities.

The Carousel House is a radial building designed to blend the interior experience with the exterior environment. The structure is used year-round, and twelve steel and glass bifold doors—each fourteen feet high and independently operable—allow flexibility in passive temperature control. A surface design on the doors was derived from a study of wave patterns—common to both the movement of the carousel ride and its location on the Peconic Bay.

The Camera Obscura is a rare program with significant historical and scientific underpinnings. The "darkroom" utilizes a mirror and lens to project exterior imagery into the dark interior chamber. The building is composed of 2,300 individual and unique structural components, which were three-dimensionally modeled, laser-cut, and labeled as a kit of parts to be fully assembled on-site. The building's innovative construction techniques, materials, and spatial clarity function as a complement to the phenomenal experience of a camera obscura.

Mitchell Park provides access to two deep-water piers supporting tall ships, ferry service to Plum Island, and a floating marina for sixty-two transient vessels. The marina program is augmented by the Harbormaster House, situated at the easternmost edge of the site. This building provides the public with restroom/shower facilities, an information kiosk, a harbor management center, and an elevated outdoor bar that engages the Mitchell Park panorama with the neighboring islands. The Harbormaster House is the literal and figurative termination of Mitchell Park's harbor walk. The park's paths and boardwalk spanning west to east wrap and unfold, resulting in the harbormaster's observation deck. This unique vantage point offers repose and views of the paths, links, and architectural programs that form Mitchell Park.

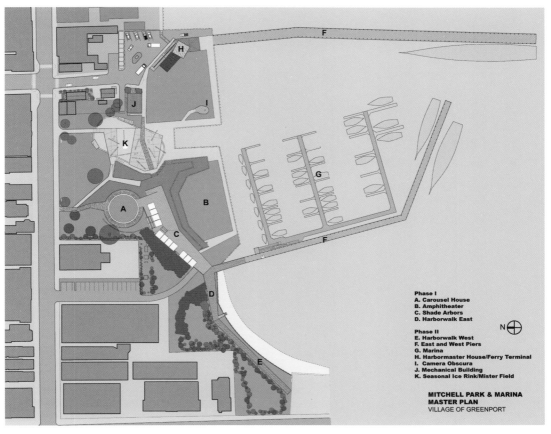

Phase I
A. Carousel House
B. Amphitheater
C. Shade Arbors
D. Harborwalk East

Phase II
E. Harborwalk West
F. East and West Piers
G. Marina
H. Harbormaster House/Ferry Terminal
I. Camera Obscura
J. Mechanical Building
K. Seasonal Ice Rink/Mister Field

N

**MITCHELL PARK & MARINA
MASTER PLAN**
VILLAGE OF GREENPORT

DELIGHT

STUDIO OLAFUR ELIASSON:
THE NEW YORK CITY WATERFALLS
NEW YORK, NEW YORK

Program

Olafur Eliasson's *The New York City Waterfalls* consisted of four monumental, temporary, man-made waterfalls, sited at four different points on New York's historic harbor: at the Brooklyn anchorage of the Brooklyn Bridge, between Piers 4 and 5 in Brooklyn, on Pier 35 in Lower Manhattan, and on the north shore of Governors Island. The waterfalls were intended to highlight New York's natural environment alongside the city's industrial and commercial landscape. In particular, the project aimed to call attention to the viewer's relationship to the riverfront, and to the way it has been and is currently being developed, experienced, and used.

Solution

The New York City Waterfalls attracted approximately 1.4 million people to New York's waterfront between June 26 and October 13, 2008, creating a unique way for people to interact with the city through viewing a work of art, both collectively and individually. Viewers were able to experience the waterfalls in a number of ways, including from suggested vantage points along the shore and "biking the falls," as well as from dedicated ferry and boat routes in the East River. According to a survey, 23 percent of the viewers made their first trip to the Lower Manhattan or Brooklyn waterfronts to see this monumental public art project. Additionally, the Public Art Fund joined with government agencies and environmental organizations to develop New York City's first K–12 curriculum on public art, using *The New York City Waterfalls* as a model. A description of the project by Eliasson was also available by dialing the city's 311 information hotline.

The waterfalls were designed with the utmost consideration for local environmental and ecological concerns: intake filter pools and special pumps beneath the water protected fish and aquatic life; the waterfalls were run using electricity generated from renewable resources; and at night they were lit with LED lights. Following the project's conclusion, 90 percent of the materials of *The New York City Waterfalls* were reused in other construction projects, allowing parts of the work to live on.

DELIGHT

Image credits

INTRODUCTION

Moskow Linn Architects (9), Fred Gurner (10 bottom), Margot Lystra and Phoebe Schenker for Public Architecture (11)

SERVICE

Marsupial Bridge: Bloom Consultants (17 bottom left), Jim Brozek (17 top, 19 top), La Dallman (15, 16, 17 bottom right, 18, 19 bottom)

Zipcar Dispenser: Moskow Linn Architects (21-23)

SuperNatural: Howard Ursuliak (25, 27 bottom), Ground (26, 27 top)

Day Labor Station: Margot Lystra and Phoebe Schenker for Public Architecture (29 top, 30, 31 top), Francesco Fanfani for Public Architecture (29 bottom), Public Architecture (31 bottom), HOK for Public Architecture (33 top), Elena Dorfman Photography (32), Albert Vecerka Photography/Esto Photographics (33 bottom)

Rolling Bridge: Heatherwick Studio (35-37)

TigerTrap: Rogers Marvel Architects (39-41)

Ecoboulevard: Ecosistema Urbano Arquitectos (43-49)

Dewey Square MBTA Head Houses: Steven Poon (51, 53), Machado and Silvetti Associates (52)

Light Rooms and paraSOL: DesignLAB (55-57)

Urban Nebula: Luke Hayes (59-63)

River Genie: Moskow Linn Architects (65)

White Limousine Yatai: Atelier Bow-Wow (67)

Temporary Event Complex: Sally Schoolmaster (69, 70), Boora (71)

City-Pissoir: Archive of Josef Paul Kleihues (73)

Urban Hookah: Moskow Linn Architects (75-77)

Caltrans District 7 Headquarters Public Plaza: Morphosis (79-81)

MVG Retail Pavilions: Midwest Architecture Studio (83)

City Street Walk: Julie Snow, Matthew Kreilich, and student work by Jesse Bauldry (85-87)

Union Square Performance Area: Studio Luz (89)

The High Line: Patrick Hazari for James Corner Field Operations and Diller Scofidio+Renfro, courtesy the City of New York, produced by Friends of the High Line (92), James Corner Field Operations and Diller Scofidio+Renfro, courtesy the City of New York (93), James Corner Field Operations (94 middle left), Timothy Schenck (94 bottom right), Front Studio@flickr.com (95 top), pongNYC@flickr.com (95 bottom), Iwan Baan (91, 94 top, middle right, and bottom left), courtesy of Diller Scofidio+Renfro (96-97)

INSIGHT

Greeting Wall: Bunch Design (101)

Mark Dion Vivarium: Ben Benschneide (105 bottom), Owen Richards Architects (103, 104, 105 top and middle)

Facsimile: Courtesy of Diller Scofidio+Renfro (107-9)

Sidewalk Series: Masamichi Udagaawa and Sigi Moeslinger / Antenna Design (111-13)

Serpentine Gallery Pavilion 2006: Rem Koolhaas and Cecil Balmond with Arup (115-17)

TKTS Booth: Emile Wamsteker (119, 121 bottom, 122-23), Choi Rophiha (120, 121 top)

Have You Ever Been Mistaken For a...?: Courtesy of Diller Scofidio+Renfro (125)

Interim Bridges Prototype: Kennedy & Violich Architecture (127-29)

Green Coat Surface: Studio Works / B.A.S.E. (131-33)

In Pursuit of Freedom: Local Projects (135-39)

Sclera: Adjaye Associates (141-45)

Making Time Visible: Alex MacLean (148 right, 149), Peter Vanderwarker (147, 148 left)

Glass Video Gallery: Bernard Tschumi Architects (151-53)

The Art Tower: Eric Owen Moss Architects (155-57)

DELIGHT

Maximilian's Schell: Ball-Nogues Studio (163 top), Benjamin Ball (162 left bottom), Benny Chan (161, 164), Neil Cochran (162 right), Oliver Hess (162 left top), Scott Mayoral (163 bottom), Joshua White (165)

Bins and Benches: Greyworld (167)

White Noise White Light: Höweler+Yoon Architecture (169-73)

Thread City Crossing: Jeff Goldberg/Esto (175, 176 top, 177 bottom), Centerbrook Architects and Planners (176 bottom, 177 top)

Safe Zone: Stoss Landscape Urbanism (179-81)

WaterFire: Barnaby Evans (183 top, middle, and bottom left; Thomas Payne (183 bottom right)

Railings: Greyworld (185)

Parti Wall, Hanging Green: Höweler+Yoon Architecture (187-89)

Her Secret is Patience: Janet Echelman (191-93)

Canopy: Frank Oudeman (195, 197 top and middle right), Sam Dufaux (197 bottom), nArchitects (196, 197 middle left)

The Hughes Family Outdoor Theater: Alain Jaramillo (199), Anne Ditmeyer (200-1)

V365/24/7: Studio d'ARC Architects (203-5)

trueNorth: Mark Ryan Studio (207-9)

1-880 Gateway: Robert Rovira (211-13)

Mitchell Park: Seong Kwon (215, 217 bottom, 219), SHoP Architects (216, 217 top), David Joseph (218)

The New York City Waterfalls: Bernstein Associates Photographers courtesy of the Public Art Fund (221-23)